TONTO'S REVENGE

THE FAR SIDE

By GARY LARSON

The Lone Ranger, long since retired,
makes an unpleasant discovery.

TONTO'S REVENGE

Reflections on American Indian Culture and Policy

RENNARD STRICKLAND

Foreword by CHARLES F. WILKINSON

A Volume in the Calvin P. Horn Lectures in
Western History and Culture

University of New Mexico Press
Albuquerque

Library of Congress
Cataloging-in-Publication Data

Strickland, Rennard.
Tonto's revenge: reflections on American Indian
culture and policy / Rennard Strickland;
foreword by Charles F. Wilkinson.-1st ed.
p.   cm.-(Calvin P. Horn lectures in western
history and culture)
Includes index.
ISBN 0-8263-1821-5 (cloth).-
ISBN 0-8263-1822-3 (pbk.)
1. Indians of North America.
2. Indians of North America
   —Legal status, laws, etc.
I. Title.   II. Series.
E77.2.S77   1997
970.004'97—dc21   97-4874   CIP

Frontispiece: used with permission of Gary Larson, The Far Side;
Andrews and McMeel, Kansas City, Missouri.

*"The living owe it to those who no longer
can speak to tell their story for them. "*

CZESLAW MILOS

In Memory of My Brother William Strickland (1946–1989)

CONTENTS

FOREWORD

We have come, as Rennard Strickland sees it, to the end of the first generation of modern Indian policy and law. In the late 1960s, Indian people could count only a dozen or so Native lawyers. This lack was debilitating, for law is so critical to Indians. Tribes are covered by literally thousands of federal laws, many of them burdensome, others offering great opportunities. Either way, Indians desperately needed attorneys to bring justice to Indian country.

Then, in 1968, Dean Fred Hart and P. Sam Deloria spearheaded the American Indian Law Scholarship Program at the University of New Mexico, featuring a special summer session for Indians about to begin law school. The program, a primary impetus for the burgeoning number of Indian lawyers, helped jump-start modern Indian law, which brought many favorable court decisions and federal statutes.

As Strickland emphasizes in this book, Indian law must be judged not on the words of Supreme Court opinions, pleasing though they may read to a lawyer's eye. Rather, the proof lies in how the words are applied in Indian country: have they brought actual good to actual people in Indian country?

Judged by that standard, the first generation has done well. Nearly every tribe has made headway, often of historic dimensions, in health, education, housing, the quality of tribal justice and administrative systems, and economic well-being. Serious problems remain, but the progress is palpable.

Strickland, however, is more concerned about the next generation of modern Indian law and policy. A poignant moment took place when a young Indian lawyer asked Strickland why the "old guys" failed to do more. Strickland, rather than defending the work to date, urged the young man on, saying that, yes, much more still needs to be done.

That forward-looking spirit is the hallmark of *Tonto's Revenge*. Strickland brings an extraordinarily deep and diverse background to bear on Indian matters. His nearly thirty books, authored or co-authored, include *Fire and Spirits*, the classic jurisprudential study of Cherokee law; *A Trumpet of our Own*, the award-winning biography of John Rollin Ridge, the Cherokee lawyer; the recent revision (which he edited) of *Felix S. Cohen's Handbook of Federal Indian Law*, the standard treatise in the field; *Shared Visions* and two other books on Indian art; and four books in his *Indian Spirit Tales* series. We have long seen Strickland as historian, lawyer, ethnologist, and art critic. To that list we can now add philosopher.

In speaking to the young people who will shape the next generation, Strickland urges them not to think of sovereignty as a ghost shirt. Fight for sovereignty, but fight for it as a reality, not as an abstraction. Bring a real, working sovereignty home to Indian country. "For law," Strickland writes, "is organic. Law is part of a time and a place, the product of a specific time and an actual place."

This will often mean negotiating pragmatic agreements with non-Indian institutions. Certain matters remain wholly internal, but in many instances the edges of Indian sovereignty touch states, counties, cities, and businesses. Negotiations by sovereigns, when they are done with care and wisdom, are a badge of strength, not weakness, for sensible arrangements can make sovereignty more secure, more stable, and more clearly the source of many different kinds of tangible benefits.

But if Strickland believes that the next generation must capitalize on real-world alliances with non-Indians, his most urgent plea is that Indian people hew always to the transcendent truth that the greatest strength ultimately lies in Indian culture, tradition, and spirituality. The failure to understand this was the downfall of Yellow Bird, a story Strickland tells so grippingly. This is why Indian art holds such importance, for, as Strickland shows, art is a main place where the Indian worldview, always changing yet always steady in its essence, is on grand display. This applies even to movies, a passion of Strickland's, a subject he explores both critically and lovingly; he concludes with a call for support of Indian moviemakers and actors. And the value of Indian culture applies to the field of law: traditional Indian law ways fulfilled the highest ideals of justice.

Tonto's Revenge builds to its climax in "Lone Man, Walking Buffalo, and NAGPRA," Strickland's brilliant essay on the Indian worldview. He crisply and compellingly explains how the Indian way—more holistic and humanistic—is different from Anglo thinking. He shows in passionate terms why the next generation should anchor all decisions in it, not just because it is the way of Indian people, but also because it is a better way.

The heart and soul of Strickland's book, then, is his fiery belief in the worth and dignity of the Indian way. The job ahead for Indian people, in a time when American glitz seems to be overwhelming not just Indian country but the world, is to tack with ever more certitude toward the star that has always burned the brightest. The American-first-means-money-first mentality will in time pass. When it does—assuming Strickland's words for the next generation take hold—Indian people will still have in place their own history, culture, laws, art, even movies. That will make for a better world for Indians, a better world for us all.

CHARLES F. WILKINSON
Moses Lasky Professor of Law
University of Colorado

PREFACE

This book consists of seven lectures originally delivered over a period of approximately seven years. The heart of the work is the Calvin Horn Lectures presented at the University of New Mexico in the fall of 1988 under the general title *Savage Sinners and Redskinned Redeemers*. The most recent was delivered to the twentieth-anniversary celebration of United National Indian Tribal Youth (UNITY) in the summer of 1996. These lectures explore aspects of Indian law, literature, art, and culture. While the lectures have been revised to reflect recent events and to include updated statistical materials, they remain essentially as delivered. The lectures reflect more than five hundred years of long running themes that seem to change very little from century to century, much less from decade to decade. An Afterword tries to draw together the author's personal observations about the past and future not only for Indian people but for all of society.

The delivery of this manuscript required the exorcism of personal devils. As reflected in the dedication, the preparation of the edited version of the book came at the time of the death of my younger brother Bill. I simply could not make myself return to this book. Only after I came to understand the opening lecture on John Rollin Ridge in the context of his death was I able to complete the revised written versions of the public lectures.

The original spoken style of an oral presentation has been retained wherever possible, although slight modification has been necessary because two of the original Calvin Horn lectures on film and on painters included slide presentations. As public lectures, these works were designed so that the hearer could synthesize and summarize the author's thoughts on a wide range of topics. They are thus described in the subtitle as "Reflections."

In addition to the four original Calvin Horn lectures, I have added three other closely related public presentations. These include the dedicatory address at the reopening of the Cherokee National Capitol Building in Tahlequah, Oklahoma; a plea for understanding and action under the federal legislation on repatriation of human skeletal remains and cultural patrimony, originally prepared for the Oklahoma Indian Sovereignty Symposium; and my speech at the UNITY celebration in June 1996. The Afterword draws upon a formal address delivered to the National Congress of American Indians (NCAI) on October 12, 1992.

A collection of works such as *Tonto's Revenge* is cumulative and reflects a lifetime of influences. Before Bill died, I had intended to dedicate this book to Fred Hart, former New Mexico law school dean, who founded the summer session that became the American Indian Law Scholarship Program; and to P. Sam Deloria, who shaped and continues to direct the American Indian Law Center at New Mexico. I know that both will understand the change; Sam especially because of the recent tragic events that have overtaken his life as Bill's death did mine.

These lectures received the help of numerous individuals, especially a series of student editors who have worked with various earlier versions presented in paper symposia, law reviews, and minority law forums, not to mention film festivals and museum openings. All earlier versions of these lectures are formally set forth on the acknowledgments page, but I want to thank those student editors and the many friends and colleagues who helped shape the ideas in these lectures. My indomitable executive assistant and Oklahoma City University Law School Director of Special Projects, Janis Pratt Young, has been central to this book as she has been to all my work over the last six years.

Finally, I want to thank my family, particularly my sister and brother-in-law Janet and Bradley Gambill, my mother Adell Tucker Strickland, and my "oldest and dearest friends" Anne and Wayne Morgan, who all worked our way through this ordeal. They understand that this book is my testimonial in celebration of a bright life cut far too short.

RENNARD STRICKLAND

ACKNOWLEDGMENTS

Portions of these lectures have appeared in various forms, and grateful permission is acknowledged for the following:

Magic Images: Contemporary Native American Art, with Edwin Wade. Norman: University of Oklahoma Press, 1982.

Bodmer and Buffalo Bill at the Bijou: Hollywood Images and Indian Realities. Dallas: The DeGoyler Library, Exhibition Publications Series, Southern Methodist University, 1989.

"Coyote Goes Hollywood: Native American Images on Film," *Native Peoples Magazine* (Spring 1989).

"If Indians Should Stage a White Man's Play: Part II—Coyote Goes Hollywood," *Native Peoples Magazine* (Fall 1989).

"Implementing the National Policy of Understanding, Preserving, and Safeguarding the Heritage of Indian Peoples and Native Hawaiians: Human Rights, Sacred Objects, and Cultural Patrimony," *Arizona State Law Journal* 24 (1992), 175.

"John Rollin Ridge: California's First American Indian Lawyer," *Tulsa Law Journal* 29 (1993).

"Strangers in a Strange Land: A Historical Perspective of the Columbus Quincentenary," *St. John's Journal of Legal Commentary* 7 (1992), 571.

"To Do the Right Thing: Reaffirming Cherokee Traditions of Justice Under Law," *American Indian Law Review* 17 (1992).

"Where Have All the Blue Deer Gone: Contemporary Native American Paintings," *Native American Art Magazine* 36 (Winter 1985).

"You Can't Rollerskate in a Buffalo Herd Even If You Have All the Medicine: Some Thoughts on Indian Law and Lawyering," 1989 *Harvard Indian Law Symposium* 3 (1990). Cambridge: Harvard Law School, 1990.

"The Absurd Ballet of American Indian Policy or Indian Struggling with Ape on Tropical Landscape," *Maine Law Review* 31 (1979), 213.

"Friends and Enemies of the American Indian," *American Indian Law Review* 3 (1975), 313.

"Inventing the American Indian Doll: Observations of an Indian Lawyer About Law and Native Americans," *Virginia Law School Report* 5 (1981), 6.

"Take Us By the Hand: Challenges of Becoming an Indian Lawyer," *American Indian Law Review* 2 (1974), 47.

CHAPTER ONE

YELLOW BIRD'S SONG

The Dilemma of an Indian Lawyer and Poet

Willa Cather, the American novelist, observed that there are only two or three stories and they go on happening as if they have never happened before. I want us to look at a dramatic variation of one of those stories—the life of Yellow Bird, or John Rollin Ridge. Ridge was the first Native American to be licensed to practice law in a state jurisdiction and the first writer of any race to be named California's "poet laureate." If it is true, as Emerson asserted, that there is "no history; only biography," the life story of Ridge is a textbook for all of us. There are lessons from Yellow Bird's life that have particular relevance not only for the contemporary Native American but for all the "others" in our society.[1]

Yellow Bird, or John Rollin Ridge, was born in 1827 in the old Cherokee Nation in Georgia. He died in 1867 in Grass Valley, California. The forty years between are so improbable that had a novelist like Willa Cather concocted his life, no one would believe it. The events of this life are dramatic. Young Ridge witnessed the brutal assassination of his father, later killed another Cherokee in a duel, fled to California, worked as a trapper, miner, and trader, studied law, wrote a classic novel, edited several newspapers, became an active Democrat politician, and finally represented Southern Cherokee interests in negotiations following the American Civil War.

Yellow Bird was, by blood, one-half Cherokee. His grandfather, Major Ridge, was a fullblood traditionalist who became the most influential figure in the early tribal acculturation process and the most widely respected orator in his nation. The family name Ridge came from an incident in 1803 when the grandfather was a young man. United States' agents came among his people asking the tribe to sign "one last treaty—a final land cession agreement." He argued eloquently against signing. "They will be back. This is not the last treaty," the young warrior argued to a council of elders. "They will be back." The tribe signed the treaty and, sure enough, when they came back the very next year for another land cession, the orator was renamed, in the Indian way, "The Ridge" because he could see into the future, as if he stood on a ridge looking toward tomorrow.[2]

Rollin Ridge's maternal family was of New England Puritan stock. His Northrup grandfather was a graduate of Yale University and associated with the Cornwall Indian Mission School in Connecticut. The marriage of Rollin's father, John Ridge, and his mother, Sara Bird Northrup, was opposed by both families. It so scandalized the Yankee "do-gooders" that the couple was hung in effigy and the Indian mission school closed rather than face the scandal.[3]

Born in 1827 in the Cherokee Nation, in what is now the state of Georgia, Yellow Bird's early idyllic Indian boyhood contrasts sharply with the violence of his young manhood and the frustration of his professional careers. Rollin's birth coincided almost exactly with the heightening Indian removal drama, culminating in the "Trail of Tears." And yet the young boy was miraculously sheltered by his father from much of this unrest, at least while the tribe remained in Georgia. During his California exile years, Ridge vividly recalled the happiness of those Indian days.

Both Ridge's father and grandfather were eloquent spokesmen for the Indian. His father, John Ridge, with a cousin, Elias Boudinot, travelled extensively in the North—speaking in Boston, Philadelphia, and Providence—building support for the Indian cause. With the election of Andrew Jackson as president and the discovery of gold on tribal territory, the life of the Cherokee was forever changed. The tribe campaigned to enlist white support in opposition to Jackson's Indian Removal Act of 1829. More than one million white Americans petitioned Congress in opposition to Indian removal. Nonetheless, Jackson persisted and Georgia continued to confiscate Indian lands, prohibit Indians from testifying in court, and banish friendly whites living on tribal lands.[4]

The tribe presented a united front with the old fullblood Major Ridge and the young one-eighth blood John Ross standing firmly against President Jackson and the state of Georgia. The Cherokees held out great hope that the United States Supreme Court would stay Georgia's hand as the state prepared to draw, by lottery, Indian lands and hand those lands over to white citizens. The judicial process proved useless. First, in *Cherokee Nation v. Georgia*, the Court refused to hear the case because of a jurisdictional question; then, in *Worcester v. Georgia*, when the Court found for the Cherokees and declared the actions of Georgia unconstitutional, the decision of the Court remained unenforced. Jackson is purported to have said, "Marshall has made his law—now let him enforce it." It is as if President Eisenhower had sent federal troops into Little Rock to support Governor Faubus against the Supreme Court decision in *Brown v. The Board of Education*.[5]

After the Supreme Court debacle of *Worcester*, the vaunted tribal unity ended. Removal appeared inevitable and the Ridges feared that delay would bring a military exile. Such was the ultimate result with more than sixteen thousand of their number herded into stockades and driven westward on the "Trail of Tears," where more than four thousand perished. The latest study by Russell Thornton, the Indian demographer, concludes: "Over 10,000 additional Cherokees would have been alive during the period 1835 to 1840 had Cherokee removal not occurred."[6]

This conflict over removal climaxed in 1835 when a group of Cherokees signed the Treaty of New Echota, exchanging lands in Georgia for lands in the Indian Territory. The tribe faced the classic Indian dilemma. The Indian could not win. If the tribe signed the removal treaty, they surrendered their homeland and the graves of their beloved ancestors; if the tribe refused to sign, they would be driven at bayonet point away from their homeland and the graves of their beloved ancestors. The choice was no choice.

Tribal leaders, including Ridge's family and John Ross's brother, believed that voluntary removal under a new treaty, if quickly implemented, would save the agony of forced removal. Their political opposition, headed by the elected chief John Ross, characterized signing the treaty as "treason" and threatened death under a law that Major Ridge had himself authored, making the sale of lands a crime of "outlawry" and placing the signatory beyond the protection of the law. The federal government solemnly guaranteed the safety of those who endorsed the treaty, but Major Ridge said, "When I signed the treaty, I knew I had signed my death warrant."[7]

In 1836 and 1837, the Ridge or Treaty Party faction moved peacefully to what is now known as Oklahoma. The Ross party held out and were driven over the Trail of Tears in 1838 and 1839. The contrast between Ross's ragged and starving new arrivals and their fellow tribesmen, already prosperously settled into the new nation, graphically exposed party differences and revived bitter hostilities. Thus, as the Cherokees prepared for a constitutional convention in the summer of 1839, the leadership of the Ridge Treaty Party was emasculated by a group of masked men from the Ross party.

Watching the brutal assassination of his father cast a darkened shadow of revenge over the life of twelve-year-old Yellow Bird. Throughout the remainder of his days, he recounted the story. In Missouri farmhouses and California bars, he told of that tragic morning as he does in the following letter.

On the morning of the 22nd of June, 1839, about daybreak, our family was aroused from sleep by a violent noise. The doors were broken down, and the house was full of armed men. I saw my father in the hands of the assassins. He endeavored to speak to them, but they shouted and drowned his voice, for they were instructed not to listen to him for a moment, for fear they would be persuaded not to kill him. They dragged him into the yard, and prepared to murder him. Two men held him by the arms, and others by the body, while another stabbed him deliberately with a [knife] twenty-nine times. My mother rushed out to the door, but they pushed her back with their guns into the house, and prevented her egress until their act was finished. . . . My father fell to the earth, but did not immediately expire. My mother ran out to him. He raised himself on his elbow and tried to speak, but the blood flowed into his mouth and prevented him. In a few moments more he died, without speaking that last word which he wished to say. . . .

There was another blow to be dealt. Major Ridge had started on a journey the day before to Van Buren, a town on the Arkansas River, in the State of Arkansas. . . . A runner was sent with all possible speed to inform him of what had happened. The runner returned with the news that Major Ridge himself was killed.[8]

Rollin's mother, the widow Sarah Northrup Ridge, fearing for the lives of her young children, fled across the Cherokee–Arkansas border to Fayetteville. Rollin was eventually sent East to Great Barrington for schooling, but his college was cut short by illness and, one suspects, his resentment at being the poor Indian relation of his New England aunts, uncles, and cousins.

John Rollin Ridge was, throughout his life, brooding and determined, with a compelling obsession for revenge. He was strong and tall and quick. The newspaperman Horace Greeley said, "[Yellow Bird] was the handsomest man I ever saw."[9] Dashing is perhaps the right adjective, for family tradition remembers him as a favorite with the ladies. By the time Ridge's temper flared and his penchant for the duel surfaced, he was already married to Elizabeth Wilson and they had a daughter.

Ridge remembered his teenage years after his father's assassination as a time of hard riding, going back and forth across the Cherokee–Arkansas border, in the skirmishes and guerrilla warfare of the Ross–Ridge vendetta. How much of this actually occurred and how much Ridge only dreamed we do not know.

However, it is certain that he killed a pro-Ross partisan whom the family believed had been assigned the task of killing him. The story is reported in the *Arkansas Intelligencer* during 1849.

Ridge, missing his fine stallion, went to Kell's and enquired if he had been seen. "There is a *gelding*," said Kell, pointing to the animal, standing near a pool of blood. "Who made him so," said Ridge. "I did," replied K., "and am willing to stand by my deed with my life." Ridge sprang from his horse to the ground.—Kell motioned to approach, when Ridge remarked that disparity of their strength forbade that they should fight in close contest, "and," said he, drawing a pistol, "if you approach me, you will lose your life." Kell advanced. "Stand back Kell," said Ridge, "advance any farther and you die." Kell advanced, and soon laid [*sic*] dead.[10]

The Ridge family feared a partisan trial in the Cherokee Nation so Yellow Bird fled to Missouri, where he continued to agitate against the Ross faction and to plan revenge for the murder of his father and other kinsmen. Soon Ridge headed West, not East as the family hoped. Although in the old Cherokee mythology West was the way of death, the black direction, for Yellow Bird, West was the way to the newly discovered gold fields and a chance at independence. So in 1850 John Rollin Ridge joined the throngs on their way to California. And while Ridge never became rich, he fought for a place in the life and history of a new state.

With his brother Aeneas and a black slave Wacooli, Ridge started for California via the "Northern route." Arriving in "the Mormon City" on July 8, the Ridges pastured their animals and bought supplies for the last perilous leg of their exodus. Ridge's narratives of the overland journey from Salt Lake City to California are as vivid and exciting as any journals written on the trek. His reactions to the heat, the mineral dust, and the great desert are recalled in the later poetical work "The Humboldt Desert."[11]

Once in California, Ridge tried his hand at almost every trade the mining frontier offered—prospecting, trapping, and trading. Quite early he became a correspondent for the *New Orleans True Delta*, sending reports that were printed under the title "Letter From Yellow Bird—Our California Correspondent," for which he received eight dollars each. In a letter written in October of 1850, Yellow Bird records his first reactions to California—the state that was to be his home for the remainder of his life.

I was a stranger in a strange land. I knew no one, and looking at the multitude that thronged the streets, and passed each other without a friendly sign, or look of recognition even, I began to think I was in a new world, where all were strangers, and none cared to know.[12]

His next three years as a Californian are succinctly summarized in a letter to Oowatie, his Uncle Stand Watie, the only treaty chief to survive the 1839 bloodletting. The letter contains remarkable insight into the forces drawing Ridge away from California, back to the Indian nations, and those compelling him to stay.

Several years have elapsed since I left my beautiful home in the Cherokee Nation. . . . It has been a series of bad luck. I have worked harder than any slave. . . . I have tried the mines. I have tried trading. I have tried everything but to no avail, always making a living but nothing more. If I could have contented myself to remain permanently in the country, I could have succeeded . . . but I have been struggling all the time to return to the Cherokee Nation.[13]

In the next year, 1854, John Rollin Ridge secured his place in literary history with the publication of *The Life and Adventures of Joaquin Murieta: The Celebrated California Bandit*, written under his Indian name Yellow Bird. The work is the first published telling of a California Hispanic Robin Hood legend. In fact, the *Life and Adventures* is a strictly literary work—a sympathetic novel of the struggle of the Mexican-American in California. Ridge poured into this work the frustrations of his Indian life and his dreams of revenge against his father's murderers. The young Indian boy who, fifteen years earlier, had witnessed the knife murder of his father acted out his own desire for revenge through the Hispanic patriot who had similarly witnessed the hanging of his brother and the degradation of his sweetheart, and been himself publicly whipped. Critics have long felt that "in having Joaquin achieve his revenge by wiping out his degraders one by one, Ridge was vicariously blotting out the assassins who had held and driven the knife into the body of his father." He put into his book all of the feelings that lay below the surface of the civilized editor. In the novel, Yellow Bird acknowledges the universality of oppression among America's Indian and Hispanic peoples.[14]

Only two known copies of the original edition of *The Life and Adventures of Joaquin Murieta* survive. But the tale has been rewritten and retold in books, plays, magazines, dime novels, operas, movies, and propaganda tracts. Like most professional writers, Ridge looked to his book to ease his always chronic financial woes. Whatever psychological relief the book's enactment of revenge brought the author, it brought him no financial relief, as Ridge noted in a desperate letter to his Uncle Stand Watie:

> I expected to have made a great deal of money off of my book . . . [but] my publishers, after selling 7,000 copies and putting the money in their pockets, fled, bursted up *tee totally* smashed, and left me, and a hundred others, to whistle for our money![15]

To insure against another financial crisis, Yellow Bird read the law and became the first Native American to practice law in the state of California. His brother, Andrew Ridge, later joined him in law practice in Grass Valley. The thought of a legal career disgusted him, but he nonetheless turned to the law. Ridge wrote his Uncle Stand:

> I will not practice the law unless I am driven to it. The general science of the law I admire—its every day practice I dislike. But for the sake of having something upon which to rely in case of necessity, I have patiently burned the midnight oil.[16]

Ridge had little respect for the legal profession as it was pursued in early California. His disgust is reflected in these early observations of mining camp lawyers.

> This part of the country abounds with lawyers . . . (whose name in every country is Legion), some good and some bad; some lawyers who understand the points of lucre, and others who deal more in monies than they do in eloquence, although the latter is not always dishonored at their hands. . . . A few are certainly such men as we can trust . . . but the majority of them, I might almost call them a mass, belong to that abominable class of knaves, idiots, and scoundrels.[17]

Ridge, like many other lawyers, was drawn into the pit of politics. On the mining frontier, democracy was acutely personal and highly dramatic. Yellow Bird could not resist the fray of Democrat (with a capital "D") politics, with its intrigue and divisiveness that on occasion made even Indian tribal politics seem civilized. You may remember that it was a fellow Cherokee of a later generation, Will Rogers, who said, "I don't belong to any organized political party, I'm a Democrat."

The rough and tumble of California politics was not enough to divert

Ridge's interest from his own Cherokee people. He wrote of a desire to return to the Indian country, and of his wish to found a Native newspaper. Ridge's Indian journal was never established, and so he continued to practice law and edit a series of California newspapers. He was the founding editor of the *Sacramento Bee* and later the political editor of the *San Francisco Herald*. Always he was an eloquent writer, spicing his journals with poems as well as unconventional news reports and unorthodox politics. "An editor is public property," Ridge proclaimed in the *Sacramento Bee*.[18] Yellow Bird remained an exiled Native with an eye on developments back in the Indian country. In 1861, the white man's Civil War became a mirror reflecting back on the old Cherokee internal civil war dating from the 1830s and the Ridge assassinations. Rollin's uncle Stand Watie (Oowatie) became a brigadier general in the Confederate army, while their old enemy John Ross vacillated back and forth between the Blue and the Gray, eventually being taken into "protective custody" and north by the Union army.

When the American Civil War ended, John Rollin Ridge was called from California to Washington to head the delegation of the Southern Cherokees who were determined to split away from their old adversaries, the Ross faction. They hoped to be recognized as a separate tribal unit, and Yellow Bird, using his best lawyering skills, fought bitterly to achieve this goal. The delegation failed. Nonetheless, they exerted a strong influence in drafting the ultimate terms of peace.

Ridge was not able to maintain harmony even within the Indian delegation, so he again left for California in the midst of internal tribal conflict. Yellow Bird's death (the cause of which we have no medical evidence) came within a year after his return to the West Coast. Wasting away at the age of forty from what was then called "brain fever," Ridge must have felt that sense of ultimate frustration he had earlier conveyed to his mother in a letter from the California gold fields: "If I can once see the [Indians] admitted into the Union as a state, then I am satisfied. Until then, whether I win laurels as a writer in a distant land, or whether I toil in the obscurity of some mountain village over the dull routine of a small legal practice . . . I will bear that holy purpose in my heart."[19]

In pondering Ridge's short but eventful life, one is aided by a little-known manuscript from his twentieth year in which he speaks of the "writer's harp" and the songs he hopes to sing. "I'll write my thoughts upon the brow of time so man may read these forever! I'll string my Harp, and sound a note that years shall echo back when I am sleeping in the grave."[20]

This early free verse tells us much, especially read in conjunction with Ridge's most widely published poem, "The Harp of Broken Strings." He writes:

A Stranger in a strange land,
Too calm to weep, too sad to smile,
I take my harp of broken strings,
A weary moment to beguile;
And tho' no hope its promise brings,
And present joy is not for me,
Still o'er that harp I love to bend,
And feel its broken melody
With all my shattered feelings blend.[21]

Ridge's letters, editorials, articles, and the treaty negotiations reveal the intensity of his devotion to the Native cause. Tragically, none of Yellow Bird's Indian plans ever materialized. Ridge's death in 1867, at the age of forty, ended his dream of "a newspaper devoted to the advocacy of Indian . . . interests." He had hoped to create "a medium . . . of defending Indian rights [and] of preserving the memories of the distinguished men of the race." The frustration surrounding Ridge's life hangs over the concluding sentence of the call for his Indian journal. "What is the use of our lying down like common men to be forgotten," he asks, "when we can just as well have a trumpet of our own, that will wake the world to listen to what we say?"[22]

On the broadest literary and legal landscape, John Rollin Ridge must be assessed a secondary figure. He is more important as America's first truly professional Indian writer than as a California newspaperman, novelist, poet, or essayist. He is equally significant as a precursor of the present-day Indian lawyer movement, but he is not a key advocate in the unfolding of Indian law. Whether with time his talent might have blossomed, with his fellow California literary pioneers Bret Harte and Mark Twain, is a matter for conjecture. It is also possible that with time Ridge might have resolved his own internal conflict and joined as an attorney in his family's famous *Cherokee Tobacco Case* or even fought the Dawes Allotment Act.[23] We simply do not know.

When we listen to the song of Yellow Bird we hear many musical themes and not a few discordant notes. He sings of two worlds. Ridge, educated in the East and by Christian missionaries, was caught in that eternal Indian dilemma. He wrote as one who believed in the virtues of "civilizing" the Indian, but at the deepest emotional level he articulated values embodied in the old traditional Native ways. The error of Ridge's analysis, like the tragedy of the Native experiences, was that the Indian could never depend upon the government itself to behave in a civilized manner.

Yellow Bird reflects the bitter experiences of his life and of many of his fellow Indians in his essay "The Melancholy of the Rain."[24]

What hopes have we not all buried, and what dreams have we not all mourned, that come to us again with the soft music of the rhythmic rain? Have we trusted and been deceived? Have we lost what we loved? Have we seen joy after joy fade in the sky of our fate! All comes to us again in sad and mournful memory as we listen to the patter of the rain.

What are the lessons of Yellow Bird? What do we hear from his "harp of broken strings"? He wished, we know, to "sound a note [to] echo back when . . . sleeping in the grave." That note is, as Yellow Bird himself understood, "a broken melody."

As I reviewed these materials, I found myself being extremely judgmental—dismissing Ridge because he behaved not as I, a late twentieth-century man, would have wanted, but as the man he was—a man of his own times. That, in a real sense, is Yellow Bird's challenge to us all—to see beyond the common wisdom of our age—to behave more like Major Ridge—to stand looking toward tomorrow.

Our Indian elders tell us that law is not just for today or even for tomorrow but for the coming generations. We are reminded of this by Oren Lyons, Faithkeeper of the Turtle Clan of the Onondaga Nation and spokesman for the Six Nations Iroquois Confederacy. "In our way of life," Lyons explains, "in our government, with every decision we make, we always keep in mind the Seventh Generation to come. It's our job to see that the people coming ahead, the generations still unborn, have a world no worse than ours—and hopefully better."[25]

This is the special burden placed upon those of us trained in the law. Yellow Bird illustrates that being a lawyer makes one no more or less an Indian. It is what one does with the law that matters. Going to law school—indeed, excelling in the law—gives us a tool, nothing more. It makes us no more nor less than the person we are. Sam Deloria, the Sioux director of New Mexico's American Indian Law Center, reminds prospective lawyers of this in a very humbling way when he tells the incoming classes in the Special Indian Law Summer Scholarship Program: "Don't worry! Studying to be a lawyer won't change you into something you aren't already. Remember when your cousin went away to the BIA auto mechanics school, he didn't come back a 1946 Ford did he?"[26]

Ridge never seemed sure of who he was or of his role. Our hero spent a lifetime hating and dreaming—questioning the Indian boy who was Yellow Bird and doubting the Indian man who was lawyer and poet. In the process, he missed the real villains and sought revenge against others who were as much victims as he. Thereby, he lost the strength, the beauty, and the support of his

Indian self. His people lost a leader of great talent and determination. Ridge was unable, or unwilling, to draw upon the heritage that might have sustained him. Yellow Bird reflects a tragic dichotomy between Indian policy and Indian reality as well as an internal dilemma that faced the educated nineteenth-century Indian. Earlier, Ridge's tribesmen determined that their only chance to survive as an Indian Nation required adaptation of elements from white society. The Cherokee succeeded in strengthening their government and creating a viable economy. Ironically, in this strengthening process they sowed the seeds of Georgia's lust and provided ammunition for her argument that no sovereign Indian government should exist within the boundaries of a state.

Yellow Bird found that there was no place for "civilized Indians" even though the "civilization" of the Indian was at the heart of American Indian policy. John Rollin Ridge was driven into white society, escaped into what later generations of Indian policymakers would call the "mainstream." And yet Ridge remained loyal to his people, looking longingly toward the Indian Territory as later generations of urban Indians resettled by postwar government policy in California would look homeward to the Hopi or the Navajo or the Blackfoot reservation.

Ridge was so caught in the immediate events of his life, by his desire for revenge, that he never understood that the cause of his people's exile, his family's tragedy, and his fate as "a stranger in a strange land" was not his fellow Cherokees—not even his bitter enemy John Ross and his followers. The cause was the United States, which forced an impossible choice upon Major Ridge and his family and upon John Ross and their tribe. Alexis de Tocqueville captured this in *Democracy in America*. The nineteenth-century French observer noted, "Destitution has driven these unfortunate Indians to civilization and oppression now drives them back to Barbarism." "If they continue barbarous," he explained, "they are forced to retire; if they attempt to civilize themselves, the contact of a more civilized community subjects them to oppression and destitution. They perish if they continue to wander from waste to waste, and if they attempt to settle they still must perish."[27]

The message for Indian law and Indian lawyers is that Native peoples must remain true to their own spirit, their own traditions, and their own values. The real lesson is the one that Yellow Bird's grandfather, Major Ridge, symbolizes: You cannot remake yourself in the image of your oppressor. Old Ridge understood: the man will be back, asking you to re-create yourself in yet another image. There is never a last treaty or a last demand. And if you change too much, there is little worthy of saving.

From Yellow Bird's tragic exile we can learn a lesson of survival. The lesson of building and rebuilding one's own civilization, of changing while remaining true to basic values, regardless of the nature of that change. At the heart of those values is an understanding and appreciation of the timeless—of family, of clan, of tribe, of friends, of place, of season, and of the earth. It is a lesson that American civilization has yet to learn.

Yellow Bird's dilemma is not just an arcane historic issue—nor is it just an Indian question. Recently, in the midst of a great controversy between our thirty-eight Oklahoma Indian tribes and the Oklahoma Tax Commission, I received a note from Wilma Mankiller, then Principal Chief of the Cherokee Nation. Chief Mankiller, an Oklahoma Indian raised in the Bay Area, commented upon aspects of this "dark spirit" of which Ridge so often spoke. "That oppressed people internalize their oppressors is a well-known fact," she begins. "A discussion of the trauma [Indian] people suffered since the first encounter with Europeans would [help us] understand why some . . . felt the need to deny their own sense of self and internalize their oppressor. A blame the victim approach . . . does little to further an understanding of the complex issues . . ."[28]

I had long thought—and frequently written—about this from the coldly academic perspective of an over-achieving, some would say arrogant, mixed-blood law professor of Osage and Cherokee heritage. Not too many summers ago, all of that came to an end when my brother took his own life. We know statistically that Native Americans have extremely high suicide rates: In some Indian communities, among children, it is one thousand times greater than the national average. But my brother Bill was not a statistic—he was a successful Ph.D., chair of the Speech and Theater Department at the University of South Carolina, a prosperous consultant to Fortune 500 companies, and a very clever and charming man. Yet one day he came home from his office, closed the garage door, and started the engine of his car.

I thought of Yellow Bird as mother and I flew to South Carolina. At his funeral there was no cedar. There were no tribal prayers. There was no mention that this was an Oklahoman of Indian heritage. For whatever reason, he had cut himself off from his traditional roots and when sustenance was needed—for whatever reason—there was nothing there to draw upon.

This, I believe, is a theme of Yellow Bird's song—we are who we are; to deny ourselves—to forget who we are—is to condemn ourselves to a spiritual, if not actual, death. The exiled Ridge, despite his efforts to remake himself, remained very much the young Yellow Bird of the idyllic Cherokee Georgia woods. If we have lost our sense of self, our cultural heritage—now is not too soon to reassert it.

The fall after Bill died I was invited to be a keynote speaker at the American Indian Law Conference at Harvard Law School. I was asked to speak about an "agenda for the twenty-first century Indian lawyer." I suggested:

One of the principal tasks of the next generation in Indian law is to rise above sovereignty and to forge alliances with others in our society. . . . There are common questions and common concerns, indeed common answers which we will never have the opportunity to explore if we do not reach out to others, to the other others, especially here at home.[29]

As students of Indian law, we know there are legal distinctions based upon treaty and statute that set "Indian Rights" apart from "civil rights." Nonetheless, we share much with other groups demanding basic human rights. Phil Lujan, the Kiowa/Taos lawyer, has a saying, "If we Indians aren't careful we'll *unique* ourselves out of existence." Like Yellow Bird, we are caught in the immediacy of our own crisis. We lose sight of the common victimizer and turn on other victims. Until we learn what unites all of us, we will remain dangerously divided.

Long before Ridge fought Ross, Indians battled each other. As tribal people, we often forget what we share. Yellow Bird spent more than half his life living in California, amidst one of the richest Native heritages on this continent, and never forged an alliance or extended more than a sympathetic editorial to his fellow California Natives. In fact, he was often patronizing of other Indian peoples.

Although I can't speak personally to the question, surely this internal divisiveness of Indian people isn't true of other groups? Not of the black or Latino or gay or lesbian or Jewish or women's community? Well—somehow I suspect this internal conflict *is* found among all of our tribes who are euphemistically known as "diverse"—true of the many kept down by society's message of self-hate, loathing, and inadequacy—the curse of "otherness."

Oscar Ameringer, the controversial journalist, early recognized the common plight of what he called America's migratory peoples—the Indian driven from homelands on "trails of tears," newly arriving Jews embarking from Ellis Island, blacks heading North on the great train ironically known as "the Chicken Bone Express," the Asians brought to build the railroads, the Hispanic following the crops, and the Okies of the Dust Bowl. Ameringer spoke of the endless trek of the yeomen descendants of the common soldier, from Valley Forge to California migrant camps.[30] Today, Ameringer would add, I am sure, the army of homeless—the divorcée from Cleveland living with two children in the back of her broken-down station wagon on a parking lot in Reno, or the gay from El Reno, Oklahoma, come to San Francisco to escape his "aloneness."

Precisely one hundred years separate the forced migration of Ridge's fellow Indian tribesmen over the "Trail of Tears" from Steinbeck's families on the westward trek in *The Grapes of Wrath*. In many ways the experiences were the same. I had no idea how much they overlapped until I learned of Florence

Thompson, who in 1936 was a thirty-two-year-old mother of six, recently wid-
owed. Dorothea Lange snapped her picture and called it "Migrant Mother."
You know that picture well. As James Gregory notes in his book *American
Exodus: The Dust Bowl Migration and Okie Culture in California (1989)*:

> Dorothea Lange . . . stumbled upon a scene of appalling proportions.
> More than a thousand people—men, women, and children—huddled
> against the rain in ragged tents and makeshift lean-tos, starving. They
> had come to San Luis Obispo . . . to pick peas, but a late frost had delayed
> the harvest. So they camped and waited. First their money had run out,
> and then the food. Ignored by local relief authorities, with nowhere to
> turn, many were now desperate.
>
> America learned about [them] through Lange's photographs, especially
> the one she called "Migrant Mother." The full-faced portrait of a gaunt,
> sunburnt woman, an infant cradled in her lap and two other children
> clinging close, touched the heart of a nation. Her face lined with worry
> and despair, this migrant madonna helped to awaken Americans to the
> plight of these particular families and thousands of others facing similar
> difficulties in Depression-torn California.[31]

But the story is even more than that—the rest of the story, as Paul Harvey
would say—is that Florence Thompson, migrant mother, was herself an Indian. She was a woman whose ancestors, a hundred years earlier, had been
driven out of Georgia and onto a similar "trail of tears." This woman, the
symbol of Dust Bowl depredation was a Native American, driven off her tribal
lands, destined to die away from her people and their homeland.

Surely, it is not surprising that this could happen in a nation built on land
stolen, or skillfully traded (to put it in the best light), from the original inhabitants. One is reminded of the cursed land described in an oft-quoted passage
from D. H. Lawrence:

> America hurts, because [the land] has a powerful disintegrative influence
> upon the white psyche. It is full of grinning, unappeased aboriginal
> demons, too, ghosts, and it . . . is tense with latent violence and re-
> sistance. . . . Yet one day the demons of America must be placated, the
> ghosts must be appeased, the Spirit of Place atoned for.[32]

We can hope that Lawrence was correct; that while "the white man's spirit
can never become as the red man's spirit, that 'white spirit' can cease to be the
opposite and the negative. . . . It can open out a new great . . . consciousness."

In concluding, I want us to return to the beginning. In my introduction I quoted Willa Cather. You remember her dictum that there are only two or three stories. The Ridge story is, in so many ways, all our stories: the story of my colleague Anita Hill, who reluctantly became a symbol of abuse by the powerful, particularly of sexual harassment of women—Anita is herself a descendant of Creek Indian slaves, tribal freedmen driven from Alabama and cheated out of their land allotment; the story of the young Naval Academy midshipman dismissed weeks before graduation, or the older army nurse given a discharge because of sexual preference; the story of Senator Inouye who was refused a haircut in San Francisco after returning from the Italian campaign as a wounded war hero; the story of the Latino family whose children have little opportunity for quality education as they follow the crops from Texas to Illinois; the story of the Japanese-American citizen imprisoned on what was Indian land in the Arizona desert; the story of the Irish-Catholic and German Jew secretly excluded because they are not "our kind."

Until we understand that our story is not an isolated one, we will all continue to be like Yellow Bird, who observed upon first arriving in California, "I was a stranger in a strange land . . . looking at the multitude that thronged the streets, and passing each other without a friendly sign, or look of recognition even, I began to think I was in a . . . world, where all were strangers and none cared to know."[33]

Yellow Bird dreamed of "a trumpet of our own" that would "wake the world to listen to what we say." Until all of us acknowledge that our songs—our stories—are very much the same, we will continue, like Yellow Bird's harpist, to play on broken strings. And yet I do believe we have a song to sing, a melody to trumpet. This need for close harmony in our chorus may be the ultimate message of Yellow Bird's song.

TONTO'S REVENGE, OR, WHO IS THAT SEMINOLE IN THE SIOUX WARBONNET? THE CINEMATIC INDIAN!

More than a decade and a half ago, the University of New Mexico's Native American Studies program, recognizing the powerful influence of film, sponsored a pioneering symposium, "American Indian Images on Film." The distinguished Indian artist Harry Fonseca created the conference poster, a rich distillation of the bizarre relationship between Hollywood and the American Indian. In this work, Fonseca's trademark coyote prances before a traditional Pueblo, the sky bright with theatrical searchlights. "Coyote [trickster]," Fonseca notes, "is portrayed as Hollywood eclectic." This portrait is not an ironic figment of the artist's rich imagination, but was, Fonseca explains, "inspired from the oral history of Acoma Pueblo when a film was made there years ago . . . [T]he old people say that the movie men almost lost their camels and ostriches when their exotic props escaped one night into the mesa canyons."[1]

This question of media image is significant for Native Americans. It transcends entertainment. It influences law. It dominates resource management. The media profoundly impacts every aspect of contemporary American Indian policy and shapes both the general cultural view of the Indian as well as Indian self-image. The power of film can be seen from the smallest details of an everyday children's game of cowboys and Indians to the international arena where a movie-star president of the United States gives Hollywood-rooted answers to Soviet students' questions about Native Americans. As John Ford's newspaperman asserts at the end of *The Man Who Shot Liberty Valance* (1962): "This is the West and when the legend becomes fact—we print the legend." Hollywood has helped create much of the Indian legend.[2]

The legend is central to the story of a beautiful short film called *Geronimo*

Jones (1970), about a young Indian boy faced with a difficult decision. Should he trade an old Indian medal his grandfather has given him for a new television set? He agonizes over the question and finally decides. The family gathers around the new electronic box and the first thing they see is the savage Indian of the movie Western. They see him again and again in the days that follow.

No group other than the Indian faces the precise situation in which their economic, political, and cultural fate is so completely in the hands of others.[3] This is so because of the way in which substantial tribal resources are held "in trust," with management and regulation, if not always operation, resting with the federal government as "trustee." The result is that non-Indians in the Congress and in the executive branch control the fate of Indian peoples and their resources when they legislate and administer practices and policies.

The media image is therefore an especially crucial and controlling one because it is that image which looms large as non-Indians decide the fate of Indian people. If the non-Indian decision maker continues to view Native people as savage survivors or happy hunters on the way to extinction, then policy will be different than it would be if the decision maker saw beyond the stereotype. In the real twentieth century, Indian people have amongst their tribal members sophisticated and highly educated doctors, lawyers, entrepreneurs, economists, managers, technologists, teachers, farmers, and engineers.

The film Indian is pervasive. No Indian reservation is too distant, no Native community too traditional to escape. The ramifications of motion pictures—social and cultural—are everywhere, international in scope. Indian-authored tales tell of childhoods spent playing at cowboys and resenting that the Indians never seem to win. My Oklahoma City University colleague historian Carter Blue Clark tells of his experience attending a cowboy and Indian film at a theater in the heart of Sioux country and observing the Indian students in the audience rooting for the cavalry as they rush to massacre the Indian warriors.

The crossing of real life and movie image is even at the heart of a debate in contemporary Native American art. Was the blue deer seen in so many Native paintings copied from Walt Disney's Bambi or vice versa? There can be no debate about the origin of a Mickey Mouse Kachina carved by a Hopi craftsman, or of the painting of a school-age Navajo showing a traditional Two Gray Hills rug with a TV set in the center of the weaving tuned to the once popular nighttime soap opera "Dynasty."

Exotic themes reflect the dominant image of the cinematic Indian. These are long-running, having begun as early as 1894 flickerings of Edison's *The Sioux Ghost Dance*. The theme that Fonseca's screen coyote parodies is at the heart of a continuing and conflicting duality. The Indian is seen as "Savage Sinner" or "Redskinned Redeemer" and often simultaneously as both. It is:

The Indian as exotic. The Indian as other. The Indian as strange, romantic, demonic, dangerous, and deceptive. The Indian as virile barbarian. The Indian as the devilish, anti-Christ. The Indian as Tonto-figure, serving his white master in the preordained task of westward expansion. The Indian offering hope of an earlier natural age to the white man enslaved by technology.

As we begin to explore the image of Native Americans in film, let us ask one key question: What would we think the Native American was like if we had only the celluloid Indian from which to reconstruct history, if our exclusive available data came from motion picture archives? For millions of people these are the only images seen. On one side we see the noble redman, the faithful Tonto-like companion. On the other side we see the Indian as ruthless pillager. We see his primary occupation as plunderer; his principal recreation as rape; and his greatest pleasure the torture and seduction of the innocent, particularly women and children. We have the Puritan view of the Indian as savage sinner, the devil incarnate, offset against the new age redskinned redeemer of attuned spirit and sound ecology. The duality dominates.

A cinematic vision of the Indian includes: the Indian as bloodthirsty and lawless savage; the Indian as enemy of progress; the Indian as tragic but inevitable victim; the Indian as lazy, fat, shiftless drunk; the Indian as oil-rich illiterate; the Indian as educated half-breed unable to live in either a white or Indian world; the Indian as nymphomaniac; the Indian as noble hero; the Indian as stoic and unemotional; the Indian as the first conservationist.

From the very beginnings some themes are almost universal. We would discover from our viewing of Natives in film that no Indian woman who marries a white man lives. Her death is preordained. We would also learn that no white man who marries an Indian woman will have a long or prosperous family relationship. It even happens to big stars like Clark Gable, Burt Lancaster, Robert Taylor, Jimmy Stewart, and Kirk Douglas.

If our Indian ethnography were based only on the Hollywood studios we would believe that the Apaches were the largest tribe in the United States. Forget that the census reports show that Navajos and Cherokees combined constitute almost 20 percent of the United States Indian population. Instead, we have scores of films with titles like *Apache Warrior* (1957), *Apache Rifle* (1955), *Apache War Smoke* (1952), not to mention *Geronimo* (1939), (1962), (1990), and *I Killed Geronimo* (1950), and perhaps the most absurd of them all, just plain *Apache* (1954), in which Apaches learn to plant corn from the Cherokees who were taught this agricultural skill by the white man. There seems to be, at least in this film, no explanation as to how the European knew this skill before he got the corn from the Indian in the first place. These whites are a remarkable people!

We would also learn from film some other unbelievable facts about Indian history, particularly about Sioux history. Next to the Apache, the Sioux have received the most screen time, in movies such as *The Great Sioux Uprising* (1953). The Sioux dominate the cavalry films and provide the standard figures of the Indian wars, such as *Chief Crazy Horse* (1955) struggling against the heroic George Armstrong Custer of *They Died with Their Boots On* (1939) and the demonic Custer of *Little Big Man* (1970). Although in the original script they started out as Cheyennes, the Native peoples of *Dances with Wolves* (1990) had become Lakotas or Sioux by the time they reached the screen.

You would think, if you relied on Indian films, that there were no tribes east of the Mississippi, none but Plains Indians, except perhaps the Mohawks, and that the country was unoccupied throughout the entire Great Lakes and central region except for an occasional savage remnant, perhaps a stray Yaqui or two who had wandered in from the Southwest. We almost never have a Chippewa or a Winnebago or a Pueblo or a Hopi or even a Navajo on the screen. The real screen danger comes from the Plains, the Cheyenne, the Kiowa (or Kee-a-wa, as John Ford's soldiers always say). And, of course, there are the Comanches who, according to screen legend, "killed more whites than any tribe in history."

In addition, we would have the most bizarre sense of geography and culture, particularly of Indian cultures. We would see the Florida Everglades–dwelling Seminoles wearing Plains feathered bonnets and battling bluecoated cavalry on desert buttes in *Seminole Uprising* (1955). But that may be balanced by *Ogallalah*, a 1912 film in which the Sioux battle their way through infested tropical swamps and Spanish moss. And the high-fashion Indians in *Captain John Smith and Pocahontas* (1953) wear velveteen and rick-rack in a kind of mod-proto-Spanish G-string. Indian dress is almost never accurate. For example, Mohawks wear nineteenth-century Navajo chiefs' blankets as early as the American Revolution.

Fonseca's poster of the Middle Eastern–clad coyote draws to mind a studio photo still used to enhance Rudolph Valentino's erotic image, showing the bare-chested, darkly mysterious silent-screen lover as an American Indian.[4] While Italian Rudolph Valentino did not live to portray Geronimo or Sitting Bull, almost every other star of dark or mysterious temperament did, as well as a sizeable number of blondes. Iron Eyes Cody recalls that even James Cagney had to line up to be sprayed to look like an Indian. A rare surviving advertising lobby card shows Cagney in a braided wig seated at a tea table in *Lady Killer* (1933). If there is one constant in the early screen portrayal of the Indian, it is that rarely was the Indian an Indian.[5] What real Indian could hope to match the stoic depth of the Indians created by Loretta Young and Don Ameche in the third screen version of *Ramona* (1936)?

There is the Oscar, the Tony, the Emmy, and the cowboy actors even have "The Silver Spur." Perhaps we should create a "Golden Tomahawk" for outstanding portrayal of an Indian by a non-Indian. The Lifetime Achievement Award goes, no doubt, to Jeff Chandler, whose early death denied us the chance to see him grow older and wiser on the screen. It is ironic, but not surprising, that Jeff Chandler was nominated for an Oscar for playing an Indian in *Broken Arrow* (1950), but the talented Creek actor Will Sampson was not nominated for *One Flew over the Cuckoo's Nest* (1975). Cochise's screen son was Rock Hudson, who started as a minor war chief in *Winchester 73* (1950) and ended up as *Taza, Son of Cochise* (1954).

There is no competition for "The Golden Tomahawk" in the actress category. Debra Paget, or Morning Star as she was known on the screen, had a monopoly on Indian-women roles in the modern era. Few could die as tragically as she. Remember her pivotal role as Jimmy Stewart's doomed Indian bride in *Broken Arrow* (1950). The honor roll of white Indians is endless. Elvis Presley is twice a half-breed. He appears in one rather good film, *Flaming Star* (1960), and one, *Stay Away Joe* (1968), so bad that one was tempted to shout: "John Wayne, where are you now that we need you?"

Most of the screen's horror figures also played Indians. Lon Chaney, Jr., menaced across the screen as a devious redman through almost three and a half centuries of frontier terror; Boris Karloff played Indians more often than he played Frankenstein, chasing Gary Cooper and Paulette Goddard toward almost certain death at the waterfalls in Cecil B. DeMille's *Unconquered* (1947).

These sinister portrayals and historic distortions date from the very beginning of the motion picture industry. The historical chronology of Indian films is relatively straightforward. The early one- and two-reeler silents were soon replaced by ten- and twelve-reelers, longer and more sophisticated films that portrayed elaborate Indian–white conflicts. The dividing line between the old-style William Ince and D. W. Griffith silents and the new silent Western epic comes with James Cruze's *The Covered Wagon* (1923), for which Colonel Tim McCoy recruited whole tribes of Indians. With *Covered Wagon*, the modern Indian/Western epic was born, followed quickly in 1924 by John Ford's heroic *The Iron Horse*. Still again, silents take on a decidedly more sophisticated look with films like MGM's *War Paint* (1926), written by McCoy and given the full gloss of the production values that made Metro famous.

Little changed with the advent of sound. *The Big Trail* (1930), the first of the talkie Western epics, failed at the box office. Despite a fortune spent on location, this super production did not capture the public imagination and therefore sentenced the genre and its star, John Wayne, to wait in the wings for John Ford. With the exception of RKO's Oscar-winning *Cimmarron* (1931), the Indian in the films of the thirties settles into the Saturday Kiddie Matinees, Poverty Row studio productions, Gene and Roy and Hoppy adventures, with only an occasional big-budget remake of something like *The Last of the Mohicans* (1936) or a Warner Brothers social-concerns film like *Massacre* (1934).

It is not until 1939, when John Ford stuns the public and the Hollywood studios with *Stagecoach*, that Indian films, or even Westerns, are once again a respectable genre. Between 1939 and 1950 big stars and big bucks are lavished on winning the West and fighting the Indians. *Broken Arrow* and *Devil's Doorway*, both 1950 releases, dramatically shift the focus of the modern Western by creating Indians who are victims, not villains. *Broken Arrow* finishes as a top grosser and sets a pattern for Indians with nobility. Jimmy Stewart, as Tom Jeffords, sounds the theme of fifties social tolerance in *Broken Arrow*. "I learned something that day" he proclaims, "Apache women cried over their sons; Apache men had a sense of fair play." Nonetheless, the old savage lingers on in "B" Westerns and even an occasional bloody "A" film.

The popular image of the Indian in the postwar Western is primarily the creation of John Ford and his star, John Wayne.[6] It was something of an understatement when Ford, at the height of the anti-Communist hysteria of the McCarthy era, stood up, squared off against Cecil B. DeMille at a meeting of the Screen Director's Guild, and said, "My name is Ford—I make Westerns." These Westerns include his famous "cavalry trilogy," all of which, thanks to VCRs, can be watched in one long Indian-fighting afternoon. Contrast these with a gentle and underrated Ford film like *Wagonmaster* (1950), in which the white conflict with the Indian is peaceably resolved, or *Cheyenne Autumn* (1964), Ford's sad failure of a film. The director says that with this film he was trying to set the record straight, since Ford felt he had killed more Indians than the entire Seventh Cavalry. Finally, there is the Ford film believed by many to be his Western masterpiece, *The Searchers* (1956), a great compendium of all of the images of the Indian, a film full of the ambiguity that shatters stereotypes.

In the late sixties change comes to Indian films. It is in response to a change in America. The Vietnam War explores itself in films about the American treatment of the Indian. It is not Jane Fonda but her ex-husband Tom Hayden who writes a book, *The Love of Possessions Is a Disease with Them* (1972), drawing the analogy between the massacres on the Northern Plains and the Southeast Asian jungles.[7] It is there on the screen in *Soldier Blue* (1970) and *Little Big Man* (1970). The Indian, in film, becomes the mirror of white society's own contemporary problems.

John O'Connor, in *The Hollywood Indian* (1980), argues that the public-order issues of the day dominate Hollywood's Indian movies.[8] For example, Warner Brothers' *Massacre* (1934) is a product of the New Deal, with the Indian as a symbol of the struggles of the new government and FDR against corruption and the Depression. By 1939 and 1940, *Drums along the Mohawk* and *They Died with Their Boots On* were intended to provide examples for a world that must be prepared to fight the Nazi savages to preserve the good civilization. So in the Vietnam era, the use of Sand Creek to stand in for My Lai is nothing new. Billy Jack, the half-breed Vietnam veteran, is simply another but later version of the Indian in the white image, as is the Indian counter-culture figure of Robert Blake in *Tell Them Willie Boy Is Here* (1969). Peter Biskind has similarly demonstrated that the Indian films of the fifties reflect the "centrist" struggle to establish postwar American foreign policy.

The Indian as savior reemerged in the 1980s and 1990s. "New agers" and "green earthers" see the spiritual and ecological balance of the idealized Native as the source of personal, if not planetary, survival. Walt Disney productions, never more than a mini-heartbeat away from any trend, released *Pocahontas* (1995) at the height of this frenzy. The song "Color of the Wind" has become something of an anthem in a popular cathedral of salvation, with the Native returned as its redskinned redeemer.[9]

Of all the Indian figures in the history of film, the most widely known is Tonto. Today, the Lone Ranger and Tonto seem mythic, almost ageless; a part of a feudal past. In truth, the masked rider and his "faithful companion" go back only to radio's pioneer days, move on to "B" serials, then television, and feature films. In the thirties, when the daring duo were brought to the screen in a Republic thriller, the French translated the title from *The Lone Ranger* to *The Bringers of Justice*.[10]

Tonto himself is the very model of the screen's "faithful Indian companion," smarter than Steppin' Fetchit and almost as clever as Charlie Chan without being inclined to spout so much ancient wisdom. Faithful companions, like other ethnic stereotypes, come in all shapes and sizes. They represent the Native American as good and noble helper, descendant of the corn-bearing redman in grade-school Thanksgiving pageants. Where would Red Ryder be without Little Beaver? Or Pa Kettle without the faithful Crowbar and Geoduck?

Let me ask, once again, why should we be concerned that the Tonto Indian of the mass media is someone or something the Native American is not? If it is nothing more than a night's adventure or a laugh or two, who cares? Howdy Doody's Princess Summerfall Winterspring meant well and his Chief Thunderthud never said anything but "Kowabunga." After all, it is only radio or television or the movies!

The media—radio, television, film—is powerful. It dominates our thinking, particularly when the viewer has little or no opportunity for firsthand observation. How many American citizens see Indians anywhere but on the screen, or recognize or acknowledge them when they do? And even then who is able to distinguish the fact from the fiction? There is a story told about the shooting of one of John Ford's epic Westerns in Monument Valley. The cameras stop. The Navajos dismount and take off their Sioux war bonnets. One of the crew says to the Indians, "that was wonderful, you did it just right." An Indian replies, "Yeah, we did it just like we saw it in the movies."[11]

Without question, the mainstream American view of the Indian is "just like we saw it in the movies." The central elements of that popular movie view are captured in the terror felt by two young boys who stumble onto a 1960s green-corn celebration of real-life modern Cherokees in Darcy O'Brien's novel *The Silver Spooner* (1981).

The boys knew little about Indians . . . but what they thought they knew was enough to make them doubt they would ever see [home] again. A. G. was convinced that Indians were generally drunk and violent, and as he passed by the big fire, it occurred to him that he might very well end up roasted in it. They would probably scalp him, cook him, and eat him or tie him to the ground on stakes and let ants devour him, or drag him around and around from a horse until he died.[12]

There is no shortage of evil Indian images in film. Attorney Chadwick Smith, former head of the Justice Department of the Cherokee Nation, has reviewed hundreds of cartoons that demean, stereotype, and ridicule Native Americans. Even the seemingly innocent are too often malevolent. Surely, no racial, ethnic, or political group has been subjected to as much or as frequent on-screen stereotyping than the Native American. There were quite literally a thousand-plus silent one- and two-reel Indian films. Michael Hilger, in his book-length filmography *The American Indian in Film* (1986), concluded that from 1910 to 1913 alone one hundred or more films about Indians appeared each year.[13] Hilger personally reviewed 830 commercially produced Indian films. This does not include the seemingly limitless "B" Western films in which the Indian was often a secondary plot figure. Forty single-spaced and double-columned pages are required to list Indian films and actors portraying Indians in Ralph and Natasha Friar's study, *The Only Good Indian: The Hollywood Gospel* (1972).[14]

Film gave light and motion to long-standing images of deeply entrenched stereotypes. The Indian in film is rooted in almost five hundred years of non-

Indian portrayals of Native Americans. Movies took the advertising posters off the barroom wall and flickered them through the nickelodeon. Budweiser's famous nineteenth-century advertising poster, *Custer's Last Fight* (1886), has been seen again and again as the climax to yet another screen version of the Battle of the Little Bighorn. The screen Indian is, with few exceptions, directly out of the Indian captivity, travel, and exploration narratives, and such stalwart literary traditions as James Fenimore Cooper and the dime novel. For example, scenes from the Ned Buntline fictional Indian-fighting adventures of Buffalo Bill are repeated almost verbatim on the screen. The transformation from Indian medicine show to Wild West show, to nickelodeon, to two-reeler, to wide-screen epic was neither as long nor as great as some students of the cinema might suspect. In fact, Buffalo Bill, the Miller Brothers, the 101 Ranch Show were all involved in making movies in the early days of the silent screen.

Cowboys and Indians joined up early on the screen's frontier trail. Many early Indian screen performers as well as film producers came directly from this whoop 'em up, wild and wooly tent-show tradition. As early as 1894 Buffalo Bill and his company paraded before Edison's Kinetoscope peep-show camera. Within a decade and a half the Buffalo Bill and Pawnee Bill Film Company was formed. The Indian film made many stops, adding picaresque novels, the Victorian melodrama, the staged spectacular, and the music hall to the Wild West show.

Even today the images of the Indian in motion pictures are virtually unchanged from early flickers like *Buck Dancer* (1898) or *Serving Rations to the Indian* (1898), or the more elaborately plotted adventures like *Kit Carson* (1903). The pioneers of the silent era left their mark as they directed Indian films. William Ince made a great reputation with his Indian pictures. From 1909 to 1912 D. W. Griffith directed a dozen or so, including *Heredity* (1912) and *Iola's Promise* (1912) with Mary Pickford as "the little Indian Maiden [who] Paid Her Debt of Gratitude" after being rescued by the white prospector from her Indian tribesmen who are about to burn her at the stake. These are all preliminary to Griffith's *The Battle at Elderbush Gulch* (1913), a pivotal film in which the Indian war begins because the savages steal Mae Marsh's two little puppies to serve up as the centerpiece of a savage banquet.[15]

Elderbush's device of the gun to the heroine's head to rescue her from the "fate worse than death" at the hands of savage redskins has often been repeated along with the admonition to "save a bullet for yourself." The most famous reprise of this scene may be in John Ford's *Stagecoach* (1939), when the cavalry trumpet blows just as the southern belle, like Lillian Gish a quarter-century earlier, is about to be "saved" by a white man's bullet.

Of course, behind all of this is that great and dominant theme of American race relations—the fear of the mixing of the bloods and the suspected in-feriority (in both equipment and technique) of the males of the dominant race. It is the "S" word—the dreaded and delightful "S-E-X" word. The Indian in film is the "forbidden fruit"—the object of desiring, the dread of fulfilling. As the cavalry escorts of Candace Bergen say to each other at the beginning of *Soldier Blue* (1970), "You know what Indians do to women?" And it was that knowledge of what they did that sustained John Wayne's seemingly endless quest for young Natalie Wood, the captive bride of Scar, in John Ford's *The Searchers* (1956).

The film image of the exotic and erotic barbarian is but an extension of what has been called the great American adolescent hangup. It is what Margaret Archuleta calls "tomahawk envy." Often the Indian film is little more than an excuse to show disguised burlesque dancing, Red Princess cheesecake, cowboy beefcake, and interracial assignations.

Of course, the Indian as fantasy fulfillment is not limited to the screen. Nubile Indian maidens and virile braves have long been a standard ingredient in the ever-popular dime novels and the modern paperback romances. Some contemporary titles include Caroline Bourne's *Falcon's Lady* (1987) and Emily Carmichael's *Autumnfire* (1987). The paperback description of *Savage Eden* (1988) is typical:

> Alone in the Kentucky wilderness, beautiful Pamela trembled under the gaze of the strong, silent red-skinned warrior—and hungered for his touch. Strong Bear was magnificent, a handsome, virile Indian chief. And to Pamela, he was the ultimate temptation. Melting in his sensual em-brace, she dared to surrender her innocence . . . body and soul. Theirs was a forbidden love, forged in a breathless rapture of mounting ecstasy. The gleam of her warrior-lover's strong bronzed arms . . . the touch of his lips and heat of his flesh . . . kindled the flames of Pamela's deepest desires.[16]

John Norman, the author of a popular do-it-yourself "guide to fulfillment" entitled *Imaginative Sex* (1974), lists the "Captured by the Indians Fantasy" among his sensual scenarios to bring excitement back into your love life.[17] The pulp and glossy magazines of all persuasions at local newsstands confirm that this red-fantasy interest continues. *Playboy, Playgirl,* and other slick periodicals regularly answers questions about Indian "love magic" and "secret customs."

The most famous of the Indian letters is one to Dear Abby. The Indian artist Richard Danay incorporates it as the centerpiece of "Kickapoos Have More Fun," a famous and highly controversial painting.[18] The letter illustrates so-ciety's fear, anxiety, and uncertainty, not to mention tomahawk envy.

Dear Abby:

I am a 35-year-old man who's in love with a beautiful 28-year-old divorcee. I want to marry her, but she keeps wanting more time to think it over.

In the meantime, she's seeing another man, and I'm afraid he has the edge on me. You see, he's part Kickapoo Indian, and I hear Indians are superior to the white man when it comes to lovemaking! Closely guarded tribal secrets on how to satisfy a woman are passed down from father to son. If there is any truth to that, I'm willing to pay whatever is necessary to find out.

Let me say that I was married for four years, and I never had any complaints from my wife, but if Indians are better lovers than white men, I would like to find out why.

Maybe your readers can help. Thank you.

Ed

The amorous exploits of the Native American have appealed not only to mainstream filmmakers but to purveyors of "dirty movies" as well. The historic filmography of the Kinsey Institute at Indiana University documents the long historic tradition of hardcore stag movies. The *X-Rated Videotape Guide* (1984) includes hardcore Indian-themed films such as *Sweet Savage* (1979), *Kate and the Indians* (1979), *Jungle Blue* (1978), and *Deep Roots* (1980). Homoerotic Indian films include *Song of the Loon* (1970), *The New Breed* (no date), and *Northwest Passage* (1988). These blatant, explicit sexploitation films for the arcade, x-rated porno theater, or the adult home-video market, are different only in degree, not kind, from a vast body of commercially produced mainstream theatrical films.[19]

The screen almost burst into flames with Jennifer Jones as half-breed Pearl Chavez. Her sultry walk captured the eye of Gregory Peck in *Duel in the Sun* (1946), a film one sharp-tongued critic called "Lust in the Dust." Gregory Peck recalled that David O. Selznick delighted in the perversity of this casting. Jennifer Jones had recently won an Oscar as the saint in *Song of Bernadette* (1943) and Peck had just played a priest in *Keys to the Kingdom* (1944). No film better illustrates the Indian as doomed sex symbol than *Duel in the Sun*.[20]

Dimitri Tiomkin recalls creating the musical score for *Duel in the Sun*. He rewrote and rewrote it. Finally, in a meeting with Selznick he said he had done all he could do or would do. In desperation, he asked the producer what he really wanted. "I want it to sound like an orgasm. It doesn't sound like an orgasm." Well, Tiomkin said, "I don't know what your orgasms sound like, but it sounds just like mine." The score stayed and judging from the reaction of the Catholic Legion of Decency it must have sounded sexual to them, too.[21]

Advertising materials of the major studios show the repressed but similarly strong impulses of other Indian films. Pandering is at the heart of Hollywood's newspaper ads, one-sheets, lobby cards, and press kits. Consider the promotion of *Apache Woman* (1955) and *Oregon Passage* (1951).[22] Hollywood believes that sex sells and the Western was, in the final analysis, a popular genre mass-produced by the studios as a sure-fire moneymaker. Even John Ford acknowledged quick profit as motivation for his cavalry trilogy. "I made four or five Westerns . . . potboilers, but they served their purpose," Ford noted. "I had to do something to put my company back on its feet."[23]

Apache Woman and *Oregon Passage* are opposite sides of the myth of the dark, mysterious, and threatening Indian. *Apache Woman* is about the dangerous, elusive, half-breed femme fatale who is shown in most ads bathing naked (of course, appropriately covered by the water). The promotional press-book takes about a half-column of print to explain that the nude bathing scene is central to the plot, while using another column to explain that it is the most daring scene filmed since Hedy Lamarr's *Ecstasy* (1933). The tag line proclaims: "Call her a half-breed and all hell breaks loose."

In contrast, *Oregon Passage* projects the image of the lusty, virile, primitive Indian buck who threatens the virtue of the gorgeous blonde settler-woman. The advertising posters for *Oregon Passage* feature the blonde with torn blouse tied to a stake while the war-bonneted, tomahawk-wielding chieftain stands stoically but menacingly to the side with tomahawk in hand. Perhaps one should not be surprised at the striking similarity between the artwork for *Oregon Passage* and the World War II–era drawing of a sinister Japanese with wire-rimmed glasses threatening a woman captive used to promote the film *Samurai*, a 1943 independent exploitation feature. After all, they both deal with national enemies. There appear to be fewer differences than one might imagine between the yellow and the red peril.

It is the repetitive regularity of the Indian image that refines and reinforces the societal stereotypes. It is an endless parade in which we have good Indians and we have bad Indians; we have "Savage Sinners" and we have "Redskinned Redeemers." In the thousands of individual films and the millions of frames in those films, we have few, if any, real Indians who are more than cardboard cutouts, who have individuality or humanity. We see little, if any, of home or village life, of the day-to-day world of Native Americans and their families.

The most absurd and insulting film Indians are those in the slapstick and romantic comedies, the cartoon and animated features, the Royal Mounted Police operettas, and musicals in which singers and dancers parade through villages created on studio sound stages. A whole generation of movie-goers seem to know by heart "I'm An Indian, Too," as sung by Betty Hutton in *Annie*

Get Your Gun (1950). The classic operetta *Rose Marie* has been through three lavish productions, starting as a retitled *Indian Love Call* in 1928, then as the quintessential Jeanette MacDonald–Nelson Eddy vehicle in 1936, and finally barely surviving in a 1954 Howard Keel–Ann Blyth technicolor extravaganza. Busby Berkeley first brought his revolutionary cinematic dance style to the screen with the dancing deco Indians in Eddie Cantor's *Whoopee!* (1930). Beautifully war-bonneted art-deco Indian maidens parade through an exotic number that is a proud precursor of such later Berkeley productions as the dancing neon violins.

From *Whoopee!* it is a quick step to Jerry Lewis with feather in his hair gyrating across the screen in *Hollywood or Bust* (1956). The Indian was something few screen comics missed. From Norma Talmadge, in a one-reeler Keystone like *The Tourist* (n.d.), to Harold Lloyd, in *Heap Big Chief* (1919). and Buster Keaton, in *Paleface* (1922), the major silent comedians all seem to have been involved with at least one Indian uprising. The screen's comic Indians rarely rise even to the level of being just plain silly. Most Indian screen comedy is juvenile and farcical, in the tradition of the barroom or the bathroom. It is mostly crude ethnic humor, often slapstick, if not moronic.

The Marx Brothers confront Indians in *Go West* (1940); Mae West and W. C. Fields get their turn in *My Little Chickadee* (1940); and Abbott and Costello's *Ride 'Em Cowboy* (1942) was originally entitled *No Indians Please*. The Three Stooges have several Indian encounters; the Bowery Boys, fallen on hard days at Monogram studios, can still spoof Westerns and thereby meet their quota of Indians in *Bowery Buckeroos* (1947). Parodies of Indians reach down even to the oldest burlesque gags with garment and outhouse humor from *Red Garters* (1954) to pink girdles in *The First Traveling Salesladies* (1956), to *Blazing Saddles* (1973). Bob Hope is often seen playing off against the Indian, with great success in *Paleface* (1948) and *Son of Paleface* (1952) and with no success in *Cancel My Reservation* (1972) and *That Certain Feeling* (1956). It would be many years before we would get a moment of genuinely rich Indian humor in Chief Dan George's death scene in *Little Big Man* (1970).

If one's knowledge of Indians were indeed limited to film viewing, there would appear to be few living twentieth-century Native peoples. The Indian would be dead. With few exceptions, the Indian of the movies is the Indian of the frontier wars. Even in the twentieth century, the screen Indian is likely to be at war, as in Tony Curtis's stoic Ira Hayes raising the flag on Iwo Jima in *The Outsider* (1961), or else a sports figure such as Robbie Benson's Olympic gold medal winner Billy Mills in *Running Brave* (1983), or even more likely the stock Indian known as "Chief" in the all-American platoon war story of *Battle Cry* (1955) or *Never So Few* (1959).

Indian films are almost always set in distant historic times, mostly the eighteenth or late nineteenth century. Films such as *One Flew over the Cuckoo's Nest* (1975), *Requiem for a Heavyweight* (1962), *Flap* (1970), and *Pow-wow Highway* (1989) are exceptions. The Indian in film is almost always a person of another time and another place. Indians are represented as dying, as a people on the road to disappearance, at best as a tragic anachronism, and at worst as drunken dinosaurs. In films, the story of the Indian is the story of *The Last Frontier* (1955). The Indian is perpetually on *The Last Hunt* (1956). He is the *Vanishing American* (1955). Even the highly sympathetic Oscar-winning *Dances with Wolves* (1990) ends with the pronouncement that soon after the end of the action these people and their villages disappeared.

In many ways, popular films continue to reflect the Indian documentary tradition. In such films, Indians are treated as ethnographic specimens with the filmmakers seeking to capture the last gasp of the dying aborigines. The photographer Edward Curtis in 1913 and 1914 produced *In the Land of the Head-hunters*, a romanticized semi-documentary about the Indians of the Pacific Northwest.[24] The re-created scene of the bear, the raven, and the wasp dancing on the prow of war canoes conveys the vitality of Indian civilization in a way few subsequent documentary or theatrical films have been able to do. Robert Flaherty's *Nanook of the North* (1922), considered by film historians as the first great screen documentary, recorded Eskimo life in its tragic and heroic modes. And even a slick commercial studio like MGM had a try at the documentary drama with their 1933 film *Eskimo*. The premise, the image, the idea behind all of these films is that the Indian is doomed.[25]

Among the very earliest commercial film enterprises about Native peoples were the traveling lecture shows that combined a "high-class" speaker with flickering films for an evening of both entertainment and enlightenment. Professional types such as Lyman Howe and "Doctor" J. A. Denton rented halls and showed features that were part of "illustrated lectures."[26] The earliest film poster featuring an American Indian dates from 1903 and advertises "Denton's Moving Pictures" at which, according to the tag line:

You Will
Be Entertained,
Instructed,
Amused
and
The Happier. . . .
You Can't Afford to Stay Away

If You Come Once
You Will Come All
The Time.

Everything First Class.
Entertaining from beginning
to finish.

The reality of the contemporary Indian's world is quite different. As the British lawyer and poet A. P. Herbert wrote, "Life ain't like in the movies." We know from the statistics that the Indian is far from vanishing. The rate of population increase among Indian people is significantly higher than the national average. On the 1990 census rolls, almost two million people declared themselves to be Native Americans. Half of the American Indian population is under twenty-one years of age. Indian communities and Indian people are alive and well. The Indian is not on the road to disappearance, but one of the fastest growing minority groups in the United States.

Today the American Indian is making a concentrated assault on film and filmmaking. Talented and aggressive Native American filmmakers are producing film and videos that portray Indians in real-world situations, using real Indians in contemporary Indian roles. The Indian is very much alive in the film industry. An earlier organization known as the American Indian Registry of the Performing Arts in Los Angeles published a directory of professional Indians as well as a handbook for non-Indian producers to help them find Indian people so that this time they can get it right. There is a new richness of Native peoples trained in the film arts—producers, directors, and actors waiting to practice their art and craft. At a recent celebration sponsored by the American Indian Heritage Association, awards were presented to Native people who had made significant contributions in the arts, particularly in film and theater. The recently established Smithsonian's National Museum of the American Indian has selected film as a key focus and has begun to host festivals and honor Indian filmmakers.

Since the earliest flickering "picture plays," the movies have presented a non-Indian view of red America. Before the turn of the century, Thomas Edison produced the first moving-picture dramas about Indians. The debate about the cinematic image and role of Native Americans in film dates from these pioneer days of silent pictures portraying "the vanishing American." More than eight decades ago, attacks on the accuracy and integrity of the white man's Indian briefly occupied the national press. Earlier, Native Americans formally protested and actors had threatened to strike, but somehow, in the summer of 1914, the cries seemed louder, and for a passing moment they drew a little of the national spotlight.[27]

The *New York Times* recorded the complaints of Alanson Skinner, a curator from the Department of Anthropology at the American Museum of Natural History. "Picture plays," Skinner asserted, "are ethnographically grotesque farces" in which "Delawares are dressed as Sioux" and "Indians of Manhattan Island . . . are . . . dwelling in skin tipis." The museum curator then asked a question that is at the heart of the emerging contemporary Native American film movement: what if Indians were to undertake production of movies? Ironically cast, his inquiry was: "If Indians should stage a white man's play, and dress the characters in Rumanian, Swiss, Turkish, English, Norwegian and Russian costumes, and place the setting in Ireland, would their pleas that they thought all Europeans alike save them from arousing our ridicule?"

The Native American perspective of Anglo society becomes a triumphant reality in a little gem of a film produced and directed by Creek Indian Bob Hicks. If there are, as many critics assert, new-wave Latino and black film movements, then Hicks's *Return of the Country* (1982) is proof that there is also a Native American movement. For *Return of the Country* is a truly important film made by an American Indian. Hicks executed this production as a thesis project at the American Film Institute in Los Angeles. In *Return of the Country*, Hicks satirizes almost every cliché of the Indian in film, from the over-heated love sequence by wig-bedecked white actors to the elaborate musical dance sequences and the late-night talk-show promotion.

A brilliant, ironic perspective dominates the sequences, done as if in a dream. *Return of the Country* turns the tables, with an Indian President of the United States and the formation of a Bureau of Caucasian Affairs, which is instructed to enforce policies to help acculturate little Anglo boys and girls into the new mainstream Indian culture. The performances of the Native American actors offset the old Hollywood stereotype of Indians as emotionless players incapable of deep, varied, and mature performances. Actor Woodrow Haney, a Seminole-Creek musician and tribal elder, infuses his role as a Native American leader with both humanity and understanding.

Films like *Return of the Country*, produced and directed by contemporary Indians, highlight in a new and entertaining way the old charges of misrepresentation leveled against the motion picture industry back in 1914, when the actor Chauncey Yellow Robe took his protest to the Society of American Indians. Yellow Robe, Sioux, was moved to action after seeing *The Indian Wars Refought* (1914), a particularly offensive production of the Buffalo Bill Cody/

Sells-Floto Circus/Essanay Company. The work, also known as *The Wars for Civilization in America* or *Buffalo Bill's Indian Wars*, is thought to have been lost or destroyed.

The Indian Wars Refought purported to be an historically accurate reenactment of the 1890 Battle of Wounded Knee, and it was widely promoted for use in the nation's schools. The producers, in fact, called themselves the Colonel W. F. Cody (Buffalo Bill) Historical Picture Company. They even employed the Indian-fighting general, Nelson Appleton Miles, as their technical advisor. Yellow Robe eloquently attacked the film's falsified, fanciful version of the Battle of Wounded Knee, establishing what is now universally conceded—that this was not a noble battle, but a tragic massacre. Yellow Robe asserted that a tragedy for his people had been mocked in the film for nothing but profits and cheap glory. Yellow Robe reminded his Indian audience that Cody and Miles "were not there when it happened but went back and became heroes for a moving picture machine."

Kevin Brownlow, the British film historian notes, "His [Yellow Robe's] audience [the Society of American Indians] laughed at his irony." Yellow Robe responded to his fellow Native Americans, saying, "You laugh, but my heart does not laugh. Women and children and old men of my people, my relatives, were massacred with machine guns by soldiers of this Christian nation while the fighting men were away. It was not a glorious battle, and I should think these two men would be glad they were not there. But no, they want to be heroes for moving pictures. You will be able to see their bravery and their hairbreadth escapes soon in your theaters."

While Yellow Robe was exposing the fraudulent *The Indian Wars Refought*, a handful of Native Americans were struggling to influence the early pioneering film industry from within. James Young Deer, Winnebago, began as an actor and continued as a director, having done his most important work, including *Yacqui Girl* (1911), before he went to France with the moviemaking company Pathe to capture the Great War on film. Unfortunately, he drifted without major assignment or opportunity until the 1930s, when he finished his career as a second-unit director on "poverty row," as the group of less-successful studios was called.

Edwin Carewe, Chickasaw, directed a number of important early Indian films, including *Ramona* (1928) and *The Trail of the Shadow* (1917). Other Native Americans involved in the production of movies included the popular Cherokee performer Will Rogers, who produced and directed many of his own feature films in his pre-Fox Studio days. Lynn Riggs, Cherokee, was a prolific playwright who wrote *Green Grow the Lilacs* (1930), which became Rodgers and Hammerstein's revolutionary musical *Oklahoma!* Earlier, Riggs had been a Hollywood screenwriter cited by Bette Davis as "one of our most important contributors."[28]

There is considerable interest within the Indian community itself in film and the treatment of Native peoples. Indian scholars have begun to write film criticism.[29] In 1980 the Indian producer/director Phil Lucas, with Robert Hagopian, created a five-part television series that explored stereotypes of Hollywood Indians. Entitled "Images of Indians," and narrated by the Muskogee Creek actor Will Sampson, the series initially was broadcast by KCTS/9 in Seattle, Washington. The individual chapters include: The Great Movie Massacre, Heathen Injuns and the Holly Gospel, How Hollywood Wins the West, The Movie Reel Indians, and Warpaint and Wigs.

None of these Native Americans, or the countless others who labored behind the scenes, seem to have significantly changed the way commercial films depict the American Indian. Hollywood has been making its own kind of Indian movies for almost a century, but those days may soon be over. Now is the time when thoughtful and determined Native Americans are remaking and replacing the old Hollywood Indian. These new filmmakers intend to banish the factitious images and bring the truth of Native American life to the screen.

Talented and dedicated Indian actors, directors, writers, cinematographers, and even producers are developing capabilities that will someday fulfill that dream.[30] Filmmakers, unlike novelists, cannot and do not work in isolation. Indeed, their interaction is important to the development of the Native American film movement. Certain key film festivals, scholarly conferences, hands-on workshops and informal gatherings have helped to create a loose network of Indian people who are serious about a creative and political Native American cinema. The annual San Francisco Film Festival is well established; the American Indian Registry of the Performing Arts in Los Angeles coordinated diverse Native American efforts in the motion picture industry.

Groups as varied as the National Museum of the American Indian, the Oklahoma City Red Earth Festival, the University of New Mexico, Artists Space of New York City and the Arizona Native American Tourism Center have sponsored events to create public awareness of Native American film and to stimulate increased Indian participation in the movie industry. For example, in one evening at a New York festival, a viewer could see Chris Spotted Elk's *Do Indians Shave?* (1974), George Burdeau's *Buffalo, Blood, Salmon and Roots* (1976), Duke Redbird's *Charley Squash Goes to Town* (1969), and George Horse Capture's *I'd Rather Be Powwowing* (1981). Each year, in early June, at the Red Earth Pow-Wow, Indian filmmakers screen their productions for Indian and non-Indian audiences.

The Hopi photographer Victor Massayesva, Jr., is among the most original creator of video films in the country. His use of historic photos and computer animation on video is an extension of his distinguished still photography. Massayesva has created a rich body of both video and conventional photographic images that draws upon the long and tragic associations of his people with the outside worlds of the anthropologist, the photographer, and the moviemaker. His video, *Hopi Ritual Clowns* (1988), is rich with startling juxtapositions of the real and the imagined. Perhaps his most striking is a film about Indian films that highlights the ironic image and continuing stereotyping. Massayesva was the first Native American to be honored by the American Film Institute, at a ceremony in New York City in the spring of 1995.[31]

Massayesva's videos are superb creations of the world of the Native American. After seeing his *Hopiit '81* (1982) or *Itam Hakim, Hopiit* (1985), the decades of Hollywood Indians seem even less than cardboard figures. One critic noted: "In his presentation of the Hopi world, Massayesva confronts what he sees as the tyranny of non-Indian approaches to documentation . . . [His] strong, almost iconic, visuals permit the audience to respond on many levels."

For almost two decades, Chris Spotted Elk made films that raise important questions. One of the most widely shown short works, *Do Indians Shave?* (1984), uses the man-on-the-street-interview technique to probe the depth of stereotypes about Native Americans; of what one reviewer called the "potpourri of inane myths, gross inaccuracies, and inadvertent slander . . . used to justify genocide, and the mindless indifference . . . that makes possible the continuing oppression of Indian people."

By contrast, Spotted Elk's *The Great Spirit in the Hole* (1983) takes the viewer inside a prison and looks at the efficacy of Native American religious practices in rebuilding the lives of a group of Indian inmates. This is a significant film that shows how cinema can be a powerful tool for displacing negative stereotypes. A number of courts and prison boards have been persuaded by this film to allow religious ceremonial freedom for Native peoples in using their traditional sweatlodges.

Gerald Vizenor, the Chippewa novelist, uses his trickster figures in a wonderful satire about contemporary white–Native American relations in the film *Harold of Orange* (1984). It is a biting attack on the symbiotic relationship of Native Americans with altruistic foundations and friends. Other innovative motion pictures like Arlene Bowman's *Navajo Talking Picture* (1986) show film and the making of film, in a Native American setting. Bowman's odyssey and the confrontation with her grandmother in the film are a revealing look at the search by contemporary Indian people to find their own place in the world.

The commercial production *House Made of Dawn* (1972) was a pioneer work of the emerging Native American film movement. With Indian actors such as Harold Littlebird, and Scott Momaday as screenwriter for this movie based on his own Pulitzer Prize–winning novel, *House Made of Dawn* captured a real sense of Indianness. Unfortunately, it did not have the support and promotion necessary to reach the audiences that the quality of the production merited. The body of these films, along with television adaptations of literary works such as *Black Elk Speaks* (1984), a production of the American Indian Theater Company of Tulsa, clearly establishes that Native Americans are now filming the real stories of their society and culture.

Today, many tribes produce their own films for educational use in schools and archives. Among tribes making films are the Utes, Creeks, Cherokees, Pimas, and Navajos. In this arena, the work of Native filmmaker Gary Robinson is noteworthy. The Creeks have been particularly effective in presenting simple and moving films of their people in the midst of the celebration of life. *The Green Corn Festival* (1982) creates a sense of the Muskogeans living a vital culture, with rituals as new as they are old. Tribal films have also provided a training ground. Bob Hicks, for example, directed four films for the Cherokee Nation before completing his highly successful *Return of the Country*.

A project informally known as "Navajos Film Themselves" was undertaken in the summer of 1966 and proved to be creative and stimulating. Sol Worth, a highly regarded communications theorist and scholar, teamed with the distinguished anthropologist and filmmaker John Adair in helping Navajos to record themselves on film. The techniques and equipment for 16-mm filming were brought to the Navajos at Pine Springs, Arizona. Young Navajos, in particular, went about focusing the cameras on their lifeways and those of their people. The result was a group of seven short documents that captured a view of Navajo people which could never have been obtained by outsiders. "Navajos Film Themselves" had a major impact on a group now called "visual anthropologists," but seemingly less influence on Native Americans as filmmakers.

Scholarly concentration on the emerging new Native American film movement does not change the fact that, to most movie audiences, the star is the center of the film. Historically, the juicy roles of playing Indians has almost always gone to white actors. This still has changed little, despite exceptional performances such as those by Will Sampson in *One Flew over the Cuckoo's Nest*, Chief Dan George in *Little Big Man* (1970), Graham Greene in *Dances with Wolves* (1990), and Wes Studi in *Geronimo* (1990). Greene was nominated for an Oscar, and Irene Bedord has recently received star treatment by film-industry press for her work on *Pocahontas* and *Crazy Horse*.[32] These days television occasionally provides continuing opportunities for Native peoples such as Larry Sellers' role in *Doctor Quinn, Medicine Woman*. The mini-series or cable movie seems to be replacing the theatrical feature film in the use of Indian talent.

Despite the dominance of "whites as Indians" since the earliest silent movie days, distinguished screen performances have come from Native peoples. At first there was Chief Dark Cloud and his wife Dove Eye Dark Cloud, and Mona Darkfeather and James Young Deer. Films like *Hiawatha* (1913) had an entirely Native American cast and were promoted as "All Indian." As with their white-actor counterparts, the names of Indian actors were changed to make them sound more romantic or powerful, and Chief or Princess was usually added for extra impact. Chief William Eagleshirt and Princess Redwing were typical names. Only a few Indian actors became well known for their roles. The most famous actors, such as Chief Big Tree, Chief Yowlachie, Chief Thunder Cloud, Iron Eyes Cody, and Jay Silverheels, appeared in hundreds of films.

The life of Molly Spotted Elk, a famed expatriate Parisian, provides unique insight into the experiences of a Penobscot Indian woman and the making of an important Hollywood film. Molly, who before going to France had been a performer in the Miller Brothers 101 Ranch Wild West Show and a dancer in Texas Guinan's clubs, was selected to play the lead in *The Silent Enemy* (1930). The film was a docudrama about three Ojibwas struggling to survive the harsh winter. Spotted Elk's diary and letters illuminate the filming and the promotion for us. In the tradition of the Wild West medicine show ballyhoo, she remembers:[33]

> Each night, a schedule was issued . . . for the next day's activities, weather permitting . . . With the beginning of daylight, and sometimes before . . . work would begin when Shorty, the night watchman, built our fires and awakened us if we were needed for the day on location . . . We donned our costumes and packed any necessary props . . . And after [we'd eaten] a well-cooked breakfast, the huskies were harnessed to our sleds, sandwiches and coffee packed on the lighter sleds and cameras on the heavier ones, and we were off . . . Traveling was difficult and slow at times on snow shoes in winter, and on foot over unblazed trails in warm weather.
>
> The scenes were shot according to the script, but when incidents arose which were not expected, they were filmed also. . . .
>
> Work did not stop with the twi-light always, for many scenes were shot at night, sometimes at [temperatures] fifty [degrees] below zero. Between scenes, the groups would huddle about camp fires . . . [drinking] coffee to stimulate them into further action. When [these night shots] were done, it was a beautiful thing to see the Indians walking in single file and hear them singing as they moved in the moonlight or deep shadows of night.

There were times when my life was in danger [such as] . . . in the opening scenes of the picture when a she-bear and I were on a cliff shelf . . . [where] the men had found the lair of [this] bear and her cubs. . . . The shelf was reached by rope ladders from below or by a narrow passage of crumbling rocks from above.

Days were spent in shooting the scene, days of climbing rope ladders and my being left on shelf with the animal. After days of mere sniffing about, the bear became really angry. It was time to shoot. My directions were to move according to the movements of the bear. . . . When she suddenly chattered her teeth at me and charged, I ran as fast as I could, but she gained on me until I felt the warm moisture of her breath on my feet. There was no place to run to for safety, and had it not been for the arrow from Long Lance's bow in that moment, I probably would have leaped from the cliff to the rocks below. The arrow struck home and the bear fell . . . with a thud.

Like cowboy movies, films about Indians are no longer the staple of the industry. *Powwow Highway* (1989) is one of the first nationally distributed commercial pictures focusing on Native Americans in the postmodern era. Produced by George Harrison and Handmade Films, their ninety-minute, R-rated adventure was able to secure major theatrical bookings. Adapted from a self-published book by novelist David Seals, Abenaki, the story is an allegory about the travels of a pair of modern-day Indians crossing the country in a broken-down 1964 Buick Wildcat named "Protector."

The cast of *Powwow Highway* is heavily Indian and features a particularly sensitive and touching performance by Gary Farmer, Mohawk, along with support from other well-known Indians such as John Trudell, Floyd Westerman, and Wes Studi. Farmer describes *Powwow Highway* as a "road movie." It is a picture of contemporary Indian life and the richness and the harshness of this environment. "It's the spiritual and political coming together," Farmer notes, "of two guys who happen to be Cheyenne and how they need each other to find the answers."

The Native American reaction to *Powwow Highway* has been strong and about as diverse as the Indian community itself. Large numbers of Native peoples have attended, and the critical response in Indian publications has been generally positive, but not unanimously so. One Phoenix-area Indian television personality gave the movie "one soggy frybread," but acknowledged that Native peoples were starving for pictures about themselves and would attend anyway. The nationally distributed Indian newspaper *Daybreak* praised the depth and believability of the actors and enthusiastically endorsed Powwow

Highway in their Spring 1989 issue. The *Daybreak* critic concluded: "This is a 'feel good' movie for Indians. They will leave the theater without anger, fear, or frustration. In this one, the Indians win. The battle is over beliefs. *Powwow Highway* lets us all share in that victory, for in seeing that there is a place for Indian spirituality in the modern world [there] is a victory for all of us." Farmer believes Indians in film and theater today are on the verge of a major spiritual reemergence, marking a sharp departure from the "Mingo-Tonto school of non-acting that set forth the stereotype." The new film movement, he asserts, will have Native Americans at the helm, from writing to advertising.

Vine Deloria, Jr., notes that there is a cyclical interest in things Indian and that the cycle seems to come back around every twenty years or so. If that is true, the Oscar-winning film *Dances with Wolves* (1990) seems to be the bugle that sounded the start of the next round.[34] Kevin Cosner's film, like *Broken Arrow* (1950) from a couple of Deloria's cycles ago, is joyfully "pro-Indian" in the sense that there is a great sympathy for the passing peoples. The production even uses Native languages and provides opportunity for lots of Native performers. A more well-intentioned production would be hard to imagine and yet many of the century old film conventions remain. The heroine is a "white captive" who is able to love the white military hero without miscegenation, the Pawnees are especially cruel, and we are told of the "end" of these people as the drama comes to a close.

Russell Means, the activist turned actor, summarizes what I believe to be a typical Indian response to *Dances with Wolves*:

I had always hated the way Indians were depicted in Hollywood. Except for a few movies with Chief Dan George, I can't recall a single film in which even one Indian character was developed as a human being. Instead, they were two-dimensional stereotypes, cardboard figures of marauding savages circling the wagons, or red Step'n Fetchits like Tonto playing second banana to white Lone Rangers. Most white people probably felt that *Dances With Wolves* was the first movie to show Indians in a sympathetic, three-dimensional way. But I thought of it as a *Lawrence of the Plains*, an overblown saga that merely substituted a new cliche for the old, the reverse side of the same racist coin. Most of its Indians were good guys, but they remained simple savages who needed a "civilized" white messiah, played by Kevin Cosner, to become their savior. The producers wouldn't chance a backlash by allowing the white hero to take an Indian wife, so his romance was with a white woman whom the Indians had raised from childhood. Once again, Indians were reduced to subhumans.

Knowing that an enormous international television audience would be

watching the Academy Awards ceremony in 1991, I had planned to bring
Indian people from around the country to the show for a big demonstration against *Dances With Wolves*. After weighing the pros and cons, however, I decided the sympathy for Indians the movie had engendered
outweighed its continued reliance on stereotypes. I also know, however,
that the same "noble savage" sentiment had served as midwife to the birth
of the Bureau of Indian Affairs. Indian people are dying of sympathy.
What we want is *respect*.[35]

Without question, the most widely viewed film about Indians ever produced is *Pocahontas* (1995), from the Disney Studios. Earlier, Disney had given
us what Native lawyer Chadwick Smith called "the most pernicious pixey
Indians" in *Peter Pan*. For those few folks who have somehow not seen *Pocahontas*, the description from the cover of the widely distributed video should
set the tone of this genuinely disturbing re-creation of history.

> Disney's most beautiful animated masterpiece brings to life a fun-filled
> adventure of hope, courage and friendship. . . . Along Virginia's lush
> tidewaters, Pocahontas, the free-spirited young daughter of Chief Pan-
> haton, wonders what adventures await "just around the riverbend." In
> sails the gold loving Governor Ratcliffe, with his pampered pug Percy and
> a shipful of English settlers—led by courageous Captain John Smith.
>
> Joined by her playful pals Meeko, a mischievous raccoon, and feisty
> hummingbird, Flit, Pocahontas relies on the lively wisdom of Grand-
> mother Willow. A chance meeting with Captain Smith leads to a friend-
> ship that will change history, as the Native Americans and English settlers
> learn to live side by side.

The most meaningful Native response to this Disney film comes from
Cornell Pewewardy, who concluded:

> The "Indian princess" stereotype is rooted in the legend of Pocahontas
> and is typically expressed through characters who are maidenly, demure
> and deeply committed to some white man (in Disney's production of
> Pocahontas' case, Captain John Smith). . . . An Anglicized Pocahontas
> who, despite a tattoo and over-the-shoulder, short dress loosely consistent
> with the sixteenth-century Algonquians depicted by John White, has a
> Barbie-doll figure, an exotic model's glamour, and an instant attraction to
> a distinctively Nordic John Smith. In short, Disney has created a market-
> able "New Age" Pocahontas to embody our millennial dreams for whole-

ness and harmony, while banishing our nightmares of savagery without and emptiness within.

Perhaps the most obvious aspect of racism in language usage in *Poca-hontas* would be terms like "savages," "heathens," "pagans," "devils," "primitive," and civilized." These terms connote something wild, primitive and inferior—loaded words to watch out for. The use of these terms in the movie implies a value judgement of white superiority. There was very little reference made to the place that such factors as greed, deceit, racism and genocide played in the historical contacts between the Indians and Jamestown settlers.[36]

As yet another non-Indian critic wrote of *Pocahontas*:

An episode historians have characterized as a genocide against the Powhatan Indians is reworked into a thrilling adventure/love story between a busty native *Babewatch*-style gal and her commanding white lover, who looks like a dancer from Chippendale's.[37]

The friends and enemies and friends as enemies theme dominates the highly honored Bruce Beresford film *Black Robe* (1991), which non-Indian critics close to unanimously praised. Indians were as unanimous in their condemnation of it as a dark and unrelenting misrepresentation of the life and history of the Natives of the Canadian wilderness. The film does raise the difficult issue of the church, missionaries, and aboriginal people, but the history in the film is wrong almost in every historical detail, in addition to being what one Native reviewer called "a deliberate exercise in vilification." Ward Churchill, in his review of *Black Robe*, raises the issue of genocide and the Holocaust metaphor. He argues:

If there is a distinction to be drawn between the Nazis' antisemitic cinema and the handling of indigenous subject matters in contemporary North America, it is that the former were designed to psychologically prepare an entire populace to accept a genocide which was on the verge of occurring. The later is pitched more to rationalizing and redeeming a process of conquest and genocide which has already transpired. *Black Robe* is thus the sort of 'sensitive' and 'mature' cinematic exposition we might have expected, had they won their war.[38]

Films of the demonic devils from the silent Indian hating epics like *The Indian Wars Reenacted* and more recent attacks such as *Black Robe* are much easier to access than the noble and highly laudatory matinees like Litefoot's wonderful toy Indian in *The Indian in the Cupboard* (1995). The performance by this Indian actor is superb and the Indian hero altogether admirable, and yet there is something deeply disturbing about the view of Indian people dependent and displayed. One non-Indian critic summarized the feelings of many Native peoples when he wrote:

> In *Indian in the Cupboard*, we see the warrior attempting to have a life based on his own culture despite the fact that in the world of the Giant White Child he's constantly threatened and exists at the whim of the child and his friends. The first shot of the child's reaction to what he has created by inserting a plastic Indian toy into his magic cupboard makes the nature of their relationship explicit: it's an enormous close-up of the godlike child's face, smiling in wonder at his "creation." And the film continuously validates this. While the warrior goes about building a house, hunting (a deer thoughtfully provided by the boy), and—almost—marrying, he depends entirely on the boy for his physical safety. The malevolent undertones of this relationship are shown in a key sequence where the boy brings back to life an elderly Native American.
>
> The use of a child as the god figure, and the fact that this is a kid's movie, serves a variety of propagandistic purposes: it gives the film an aura of sweetness, innocence, and "childlike wonder," effectively masking its subtext of the "inevitability" of the Native American as a literally vanishing character in the cultural consciousness. The warrior is seen as an acceptable historical casualty of society's "progress" and—in *The Indian in the Cupboard*, as in many cultural texts—as an important fixture in the landscape of leisure.[39]

Often when I teach the basic American Indian law course, I encourage my students to rent the videos of two Indian films—*Incident at Ogalala* (1992) and *Thunderheart* (1992). The first is a documentary directed by Michael Apted; the second is a fictionalized crime adventure about the same incident, focusing on a mixed-blood FBI agent searching for himself and for the criminal. The two films should be viewed together. Both deal with the injustice of the Leonard Peltier case and provide a quite remarkable contrast in cinematic style, but both illustrate how film can be used to get at the truth or truths. Unfortunately, neither film has moved us to a just resolution of what I personally believe to be a tragic abuse of the justice system. Both films should be available at your corner video store; I encourage you to view this double feature. I believe that after you have seen them you will ask yourself, "What can I do to help?"[40]

On a positive note, Turner Network Television (TNT) has produced five films in a series "devoted to historically accurate depictions of stories from the American Indian culture." The climatic film in the series was *Crazy Horse* (1996). Preparing the film and the series was taken seriously by a substantial number of Native Americans who were involved in the creative endeavor. "It's a long, complicated process," said producer and Kiowa filmmaker Hanay Geiogmah. "We consulted scholars, writers and cultural people within the tribes themselves to give us input, reflections, advice and guidance." This represents an effort to provide a balance. As writer and co-executive producer Robert Schenkkan notes: "*Crazy Horse* represents a set of universal ideals that everyone should be aware of. To appreciate what he stood for and his concern for the people is something we can all admire and emulate." This is a case where a network did put its money where its mouth had been and sought the talents of Indian people working in the industry. If the media is to correctly represent Native peoples, more of this is needed.[41]

I want to close what has thus far been a pessimistic review of the historic and contemporary state of the Native American in film on a note of optimism. In July of 1996, Home Box Office premiered Greg Sarris's *Grand Avenue*, a film about modern urban Indians that Native historian and novelist Michael Dorris called, in his glowing review in the *New York Times*, "a giant step toward offering a gritty and unsparing depiction of contemporary urban Indian life." Not only was the film well received by Indian people and film critics, but *Grand Avenue* earned the highest viewer ratings of any HBO show of the season.

Greg Sarris is a professor of Pomo and Miwok heritage at UCLA and served as executive producer for the film adaptation of his novel *Grand Avenue*. Co-producer Paul Aaron of the Sundance Institute (Robert Redford served as executive producer) explains that their goal was "to let contemporary Indians tell their own story." "I wanted to make a movie," producer Aaron notes, "in which there was no white character to lead us in. The characters who draw us in are Indians." This contrasts sharply with what Aaron sees in "most [Indian] movies [that] are about white characters wandering into the world of Native Americans."[42]

As we move toward the twenty-first century, there is no question that many filmmakers are increasingly concerned, indeed even sensitive, about their treatment of the American Indian. For example, ABC—Capitol Cities spent a significant amount of time and energy in preparing for their production of the Custer drama *Son of the Morning Star*. Nancy Tuthill, a distinguished American Indian lawyer, was charged with the impossible task of helping produce a "balanced script" of what I would call an "impossibly imbalanced scenario."

In truth, there may be some stories that can never be told in a "balanced" way. I wonder what Steven Spielberg would have done had he been required to "balance" *Schindler's List* (1994)? I think there is no better argument for encouraging Native people to continue developing their interest in and their skills for film. Would it be heresy for me, as a law school dean and professor, to suggest that a few more Indian filmmakers might be at least as productive a use of Indian talent? Some might argue even more so!

The current assault that Coyote is making upon the film establishment is positive. The goals are to tell—and tell truthfully—the story of the Native American. If the new wave of Indian filmmaking succeeds, then the old screen Tonto stereotypes will be gone. It can then be honestly said with pride that the vanishing Indian is the Hollywood Indian—and that the real Indian people are alive and well and living in America.

The crisis for the present-day Indian working in film is that there are relatively few major motion pictures or television series about Indians in production, a far cry from the hundreds produced in earlier years. And the day has not yet come when the industry appears willing to regularly consider these talented Native Americans in a context other than a Native American one. Today, Indians must create their own film opportunities. For example, film workshops are held to help tribes become involved in filmmaking. The Institute for American Indian Art in Santa Fe has a film-study curriculum. The Smithsonian's newly established National Museum of the American Indian sponsors festivals and workshops focusing on Indian makers of film. These activities make a significant statement of Native American recognition that film art is important. All across the country Indians are beginning to seize the opportunity to reshape their cinematic image. Self-determination is a factor in film as well as other Indian areas of choice and policy.

I close on a personal note. When I was a young boy—still in grade school—Warner Brothers came to my home town of Muskogee, Oklahoma, to make the movie *Jim Thorpe—All American* (1951). My father and mother (like another two thousand or so Oklahoma mixed-bloods) were invited to "The Jim Thorpe Reception." I went with them to see Jim Thorpe, the greatest athlete of the twentieth century. Burt Lancaster was there, along with Phyllis Thaxter, Steve Cochran, and Charles Bickford. I foolishly asked, "Where is Jim Thorpe?" Jim Thorpe was not there! I later learned that the studio paid Thorpe for screen rights, but refused to bring him along to the location because he was just "too much trouble." As Iron Eyes Cody recalls:

At the halfway mark in the twentieth century, 1950, America took a look over its shoulder. Hundreds of sports writers were polled nationwide, and the man voted the greatest athlete of the twentieth century was Jim Thorpe. . . . And, of course, Hollywood was hot on his trail again. Warner Brothers gave the okay for a million-dollar production based on his life because, as Jack Warner said, "Jim Thorpe's story could only have happened in America." He probably was right at that. Jim was given $25,000 for the rights to do his life story. Burt Lancaster and Charles Bickford were signed for the title roles . . . Then they had to come up with somebody to play Jim's father.

"Why the hell don't you let Jim play it himself," I said to director Michael Curtiz. "He'd be great!"

Curtiz frowned and looked down. "Well, actually, Iron Eyes, we were thinking of casting you. What do you say?"

"Nah, you got the wrong man. Give it to Jim. It would mean a lot to him—and think of the [box office] draw he'd be."

Curtiz balked, telling me something about Jim being too overweight and "not right." When the film crew departed for Oklahoma to shoot the opening scenes of Jim Thorpe's boyhood, they left without Jim Thorpe. Wouldn't even use him as a sports technical advisor. And I can tell you it broke his heart, visibly. The big man actually wept.[43]

That says it all. Filmmakers have been making Indian movies for more than a century now, mostly without the Indian, because the Indian is the wrong man for the part or just too much trouble. I hope those days will soon be over. We have seen what a great Indian actor like Will Sampson can do with a part like that of the Indian who must suffocate the sickness produced by the institutions of white society. Now is the time when thoughtful and determined Native Americans are flying over the cuckoo's nest that is Hollywood. Indian filmmakers and actors intend to suffocate the old images and convert the screen Indian into a real Indian. Tonto, you may yet have your revenge.

CHAPTER THREE

"YOU CAN'T ROLLERSKATE IN A BUFFALO HERD EVEN IF YOU HAVE ALL THE MEDICINE"

American Indian Law and Policy

I was recently privileged to be a "scholar in residence" at the Heard Museum, working on an international touring exhibition called "Shared Visions." Before we consider the powers and the limitations of law, I'd like to draw your attention to an important work of contemporary Native American art. One of the paintings regarded as a masterwork of Native art is George Longfish's *You Can't Rollerskate in a Buffalo Herd Even If You Have All the Medicine* (1979–80). I must confess that *You Can't Rollerskate* is one of my favorite works of modern art. It is a large, loosely gathered canvas designed to hang like an old teepee liner. From the freedom and flexibility of the linen comes a frantic movement of worlds in collision. There are storms and sun spots and lighting, discordant in action but drawn in soothing and reinforcing colors and spaces.[1] I see this as the world of modern Indian law. This is the arena in which the Indian lawyers we are educating will live and work.

Today, I want to focus on what I believe to be the challenges of those who choose to work (I hesitate to say practice) in the field of Native American law and policy. I want to look to the unique opportunities and special dangers that lie ahead for Indian law and Indian lawyers. You will have to excuse me if I seem to preach. This is something in which I believe—and believe evangelically. I am really not preaching, only professing. I discovered this year that I have been about the business of professing longer than I have not. For more than half my life now, my daily bread has been earned by talking to the next generation about the things my generation thought important. No doubt it is a very strange way to earn a living. I have been about it long enough to have come to understand, I hope, something of what the Spanish philosopher José Ortega y Gasset meant when he wrote of "the concept of generations".[2]

The great American Indian artist, the Kiowa-Caddo T. C. Cannon, reflected this same view when he painted that wry and poignant picture of the resilience of the American Indian entitled *Grandmother Gestating Father and the Washita River Runs Ribbon-Like*. It is in the meaning of the Keetoowah wampum belts read at the annual summer green corn that show the unbroken lines standing for the tribe running forward and backward, running now and forever. Ortega, in *The Modern Theme*, describes his "concept of generations"—of one generation growing out of another, building from the strengths and weaknesses of the previous one, extending and modifying, correcting and confirming. Survival is possible only through incremental growth from one generation to the next.

Whenever I am discouraged about that future survival of Indian people and Indian law, and believe me in recent years I have been mightily discouraged, I wonder how we got here. I believe we are here—all Indian people are here—because somewhere and at some time a young determined Native girl or a stubborn half-blood boy sat with tight shoes, speaking a strange tongue, in a hostile classroom when they'd rather have been out racing with the wind. This traditional strength and power is what generations before have given us. Our question is what shall our generations—my generation and yours—leave to those who will follow us along those ribbonlike rivers.

I may not be the right person to speculate about law. As I am always quick to point out, I think of myself as a student of the history of Indian law and policy, one who has never fully understood or believed in the magic of case law as a "ghost dance shirt" that will bring back the buffalo. I have seen too many of our victories won in hard-fought court battles slip away to think that law alone is enough. I believe the task over the next generation for Indian law is to sustain and extend the legal victories of the last decades while shaping, building, and fortifying those victories and others of their own creation into meaningful and workable programs. We must transform the outlines of what courts say tribes might do into things that tribes are actually doing. Our task is to actualize the theoretical, to make happen what Indian law has convinced the courts could happen.

To appreciate where we are now, we need to look back over the generations, over what in Indian law we call the "policy eras." We know the periods by a sort of shorthand such as the treaty era, the allotment era, termination, urban resettlement, and self-determination/self-governance. From a careful study of each of these eras we learn the lesson that nothing in Indian law or policy ever stays the same, that there is no time to stop and savor the trophies of victory or even to lick the wounds of defeat. The eras move too quickly, change too suddenly. Yesterday's opportunities are too often gone before we can make them real. The task of Indian law is to seize the opportunity while it is momentarily here; to act before the avenue of action is blocked.

In recent years, we have come to speak of a so-called modern legal era, which Charles Wilkinson has pointed out opens with the 1959 Supreme Court case of *Williams v. Lee*.[3] I suspect the curtain begins to descend with the *Oliphant* decision of the Supreme Court. While lawyers focus on cases, we often miss more crucial happenings in the broader world of the Indian. As we moved into the *Williams v. Lee* modern era, additional and perhaps even more important events were taking place elsewhere in Indian country.

Vine Deloria, Jr., has described the contributions of a generation of Indian leadership—young men now grown much older—who returned from the Second World War and from Korea newly energized and educated to a universe of diverse peoples. These were Indian leaders who saw beyond the narrow confines of a BIA—and missionary school—dictated world. They were ready to make things happen. And they did. They were women and men who, as Deloria notes, had read their Cohen and knew what the law was supposed to be. The possibility of redress of age-old grievances was spotlighted by the potential of the Indian Claims Commission. The kind of political, tribal, and pan-Indian social and legal activism that they created was essentially unknown before the Second World War. They made the world of modern Indian law possible.[4]

I was reminded of their achievements when I visited the Lummi in Washington State as a part of an evaluation of the Indian Self-Governance Demonstration Project. We talked with a tribal elder who recalled what tribal life was like when her husband returned from serving as a Marine sergeant in the Second World War. She vividly recreated for us the meeting at which the Bureau called the tribe together and told them the tribe was to be "terminated." The man from the BIA told them it was going to happen one of two ways: either the "easy way" with the tribe helping the Bureau make a smooth transition or the "hard way" with the Bureau doing it alone. With tears in her eyes, a tremor in her voice, and pride on her face, she reported that her previously shy husband stood up, drawing upon his military demeanor and experience said, "*No*, there is a third way and that is with the tribe saying 'NO' and, if necessary, going to the congress to stop you." As she reminded us, the Bureau controlled the budget and so those young veterans and their young brides and newborn children held bake sales and packed lunches and went to Washington on the bus. Their way ultimately became the way. The tribe survived termination and this led to many changes that culminated decades later in *U.S. v. Washington*, the Boldt decision that recognized the birth of West Coast Indian fishing rights.

Close on the heels of these veterans came another generation and another achievement that lawyers and would-be lawyers with our heads in the statute books may underestimate. The years 1968–69 mark an important and often unrecognized dividing line in the history of the Native American. Within little more than six months, white dominance of the image of the Red American came to an end. And it ended with a bang—an explosion set off by the almost simultaneous publication of three books. The books were *House Made of Dawn* (1968), a Pulitzer Prize-winning novel about the struggles of modern Indians in the postwar era; *Custer Died for Your Sins* (1969), a best-selling political tract subtitled "An Indian Manifesto"; and *The Tewa World* (1969), a critically acclaimed anthropological inquiry into the values of a Pueblo community in the present-day Southwest.

The authors—N. Scott Momaday (Kiowa-Cherokee), Vine Deloria, Jr. (Standing Rock Sioux), and Alfonso Ortiz (San Juan Pueblo)—were Native Americans who wrote with a passion, an insight, and a skill that rescued the stereotyped Indian from the dusty provinces of history. After that historic year it was no longer possible for any literate American to believe that the Indian was on a road to disappearance. They wrote of Indians who lived in a real world somewhere between the "Savage Sinner" and the "Redskinned Redeemer." Over the last three decades, these distinguished Indian authors have continued to write and have been joined by hundreds of other Native American poets, novelists, essayists, journalists, historians, and anthropologists.

If the movies created Native people who were only one-dimensional historical relics, the modern Indian writer has pictured people who are complex and contemporary while still being traditionally Indian in values and outlook. Two decades after *House Made of Dawn*, Louise Erdrich's powerful novel *Tracks* (1988), was a Book-of-the-Month Club Selection and on the *New York Times* best-seller list. Indian literature was being read by white Americans and was changing the potential of Indian life every bit as surely as were court cases.

This new Indian literature portrayed Indians as people who were alive, who were struggling, who were determined that they and their descendants would survive. This message is nowhere more eloquently proclaimed than in "The Delight Song," an early poem of Scott Momaday:

> You see, I am alive, I am alive.
> I stand in good relation to the earth.
> I stand in good relation to the gods.

I stand in good relation to all that is beautiful.
I stand in good relation to the daughter of Tsen-tainte.
You see, I am alive, I am alive.[5]

While Deloria and Momaday and Ortiz were demonstrating Indians were alive, a whole generation—including Deloria himself—heard a calling to law. Seemingly overnight, although in reality it took two decades, there was in place a cadre of legally trained Native peoples who stood ready to fight for Indian rights. And fight they did, alongside an equally dedicated generation of Anglo attorneys. As a result of the Special Scholarship Program in American Indian Law at the University of New Mexico, Native peoples were given a unique opportunity to study law. Other law schools followed course until today there are more than a thousand attorneys of Indian heritage; a generation ago there were less than a dozen.

At the same time new law delivery institutions began to emerge, ranging from programs such as the California Rural Legal Services to tribal efforts such as the Navajo's DNA, to a major public-interest legal arm like the Native American Rights Fund. Indian law and Indian lawyers had come of age. The wine was heady, the achievement mighty. There was a sense of the triumph of law in the air. Water Rights! Fishing Rights! Tribal Powers to Tax! It was a march in time to the chant of newly acknowledged tribal sovereignty. It was a good time to be young and alive and especially to be an attorney for Indians.

Over time, Indians have increasingly come to be at home with law. The Indian lawyer is no longer a stranger in a strange land. What that earlier generation, which Vine describes with such care and respect, came painstakingly to know by kerosene lamp in cold and lonely cabins, reading from a thumb-worn Cohen, we are now learning at universities—at Oklahoma City and Oregon and New Mexico and Wisconsin and the more than eighty other law schools that now teach a basic Indian law course. Not that it is easy; law is still strange and bizarre and foreign in so many ways. Whether the achievements of university-trained Indian lawyers will be as meaningful and long-lasting is another question—one upon which the jury is still out. Much of what has survived of Indian tribal values, indeed of tribal government, is a result of those Indian men and women who returned from the Second World War determined that the rivers would still flow.

The first generation of Indian lawyers are mostly their sons and daughters—women and men who have met much and early success, but who in recent years have been forced to address the fact that winter follows the autumn as surely as the summer follows the spring and that too often You Can't Roller-skate in a Buffalo Herd Even If You Have the Law. The first signs of winter came along about *Oliphant,* and the blizzard really arrived with *Lyng v. North-west Cemetery Protective Association.*[6]

At this moment, I believe the great generational challenge—the challenge of both your generation and mine—is to make Indian law work for Indian people at the most elemental human level. My generation has been listening to—indeed helping to create—the music of sovereignty. *Sovereignty!* The word slides melodically from our lips, but sovereignty alone doesn't put food on tables, clothes on backs, or heat in houses. Sovereignty is not a state of salvation that magically erases all troubles. It can be a siren's song drawing us away from the real needs of real people. Our challenge—the challenge of Indian law—is to forge the sword of sovereignty into a weapon capable of attacking the basic human problems of Indian people. So before we talk about the details of law for Native Americans, let us look at the people for whom we speak of law—the American Indian on the verge of entering the twenty-first century.[7]

The contemporary Native American is one of the fastest growing groups in the United States. The 1990 Bureau of the Census Report shows that there are now approximately two million Native Americans. More than half of this number live on or near Indian reservations, trust land, or Native villages. Approximately 90 percent of the reservation population is concentrated in eleven states. The three largest by state are Oklahoma, Arizona, and New Mexico. California, with a very large Indian population, has less than 10 percent of these on Indian land. Even the urban Indian is highly concentrated, with more than 90 percent in only fifteen states.

These statistics hide the vast diversity of life and lifestyles of the Native American. The contemporary American Indian is as varied as the Alaskan villager, the Kansas Kickapoo, the Florida Seminole, the Onondaga of New York, the Dakotas' Sioux, the New Mexico Pueblo, the Arizona Navajo, and the Oklahoma Osage. American Indians live on 278 reservations and Alaskan Natives live in 487 villages. Some groups and reservations are large. The Navajos together with the Cherokees constitute almost 20 percent of the American Indian population. And yet 35 percent of all reservations and villages have fewer than one hundred persons in residence. Nearly three-fourths of all the reservations and villages have fewer than five hundred inhabitants.

The most encouraging aspect of recent census figures is that the Indian population is young—quite young in comparison to the rest of the population. Almost a third of the Indian population is under fifteen years of age, while only about one-fifth of the non-Indian population is under fifteen. The median age for all Indians is twenty-three. Even more promising is the number of Indians enrolled in nursery, kindergarten, elementary, high school, and college. One-third of the Indian population is in school. More than half of the Indian population under twenty-five has completed high school, as compared to one-third in the older group. The median years of school completed in 1990 is up considerably from 1970.

Whatever index is chosen to measure Indian conditions, the statistics are tragic evidence of failure. The income level, health conditions, housing standards, unemployment rate, educational level, and statistics of alcoholism, crime, and juvenile delinquency all establish that "American Indians . . . suffer . . . indignities that few groups in America suffer in equal measures." An Indian born in the twentieth century will live a life not significantly longer in span than his ancestor of five hundred years ago. Although the last decade has brought considerable improvement, the Indian is still left out of many of the advances of modern medicine. The United States population as a whole will live one-third longer than the American Indian.

The Indian health level is the lowest and the disease rate the highest of all major population groups in the United States. The incidence of tuberculosis is over 400 percent higher than the national average. Similar statistics show that the incidence of strep infections is 1,000 percent, meningitis is 2,000 percent higher, and dysentery is 10,000 percent higher. Death rates from disease are shocking when Indian and non-Indian populations are compared. Influenza and pneumonia are 300 percent greater killers among Indians. Diseases such as hepatitis are at epidemic proportions, with an 800 percent higher chance of death. Diabetes is almost a plague. And the suicide rate for Indian youths ranges from 1,000 to 10,000 times higher than for non-Indian youths; Indian suicide has become epidemic. As an educated mixed-blood, you sometimes think yourself exempt from our Indian common fates. My family was struck when my younger brother took his own life. None of us can escape the realities of being Indian.

On many reservations, several generations of Indians are housed in two or three rooms that contain no plumbing or bathing facilities. Despite the substantial efforts of tribal housing authorities, between fifty thousand and fifty-seven thousand Indian homes are still considered uninhabitable. Many of these are beyond repair. For example, over 88 percent of the homes of the Sioux in Pine Ridge have been classified as substandard dwellings. More than 25 percent of all American Indians, as compared with 12.4 percent of the non-Indian population are living below the poverty level. The unemployment rate on reservations is 25.6 percent; median Indian income is 16 percent lower than the national average.

Compare this devastating poverty with the richness of undeveloped Indian resources. In his eloquent essay, "Shall the Islands Be Preserved?," Professor Wilkinson inventories some of the tribal assets:

The reservation system comprises some 52 million acres—about 2½% of the entire surface area of the United States. Add to that the forty million acres which will be transferred to Alaska natives as well as unresolved land claims in many states. . . . The tribes have large mineral holdings: 10% of the nation's coal, 10% of the oil, and a minimum of 16% of the uranium. In addition to valuable recreation land, Indians own 1½% of the country's commercial timber and 5% of the grazing land. And reservation Indians have first call on the water in many rivers in the parched western half of the country.[8]

Indian culture, like the Indian population, is very much alive. Survival is perhaps the word that best describes the spirit of Indian people as diverse as the Kiowas of the Sun Dance and the Cherokee of the Kee-Too-Wah fire. Despite dire deprivation, Indian people have learned the lesson of adapting, of changing, and yet of remaining true to basic values. Despite raw poverty and bleak economic prospects, the modern Indian glories in his Indianness. Indian pride is a contemporary reality of Native life.

Native people, particularly tribal leaders, and their lawyers take pride in the fact that Indian law is unique because of sovereignty and the "government-to-government" relationships. But I believe one of the principal tasks of the next generation in Indian law is to rise above sovereignty and to forge alliances with others in our society. Indeed, I also believe your challenge and your opportunity is worldwide and will encompass bringing the Native American into the broader struggles of indigenous peoples everywhere. There are common questions and common concerns, indeed, common answers we will never have the opportunity to explore if we do not reach out to others, to the others especially who are here at home.

A great achievement for any generation would be to enlist a broad national consciousness in support of Indian peoples. This is essential because in terms of raw numbers, of actual votes, or of crude political power—the Native American remains less than 1 percent of the total population. It is for this reason, if for no other, that law remains so central to the Indian's quest. It may be an imperfect game but, for the Indian, law may be the only game in town. It is for this reason that we celebrate the remarkable legal achievements of the Indian lawyer and Indian law in the modern era. It is for this reason that we must be dedicated to the hard task of fulfilling responsibilities that come with these recently established rights. This challenge will weigh heavily upon coming generations.

In the late 1930s and early 1940s, Felix Cohen created our field of Indian law. Cohen was our Blackstone in that he brought systematic legal order out of the chaos of Indian policy. The last fifty years, most particularly the last twenty-five, have been spent implementing the theoretical and philosophical base distilled by Cohen and his associates from the five thousand–plus laws, statutes, treaties, regulations cases, executive orders, and tribal enactments that constitute the raw material of Indian law. As should be expected and encouraged, many young Indian scholars of the coming generation are questioning and confronting Cohen's conclusions. Since *Williams v. Lee* the field of Indian law has grown and matured. While in the original Cohen *Handbook* there were only a few pages on water rights, fishing rights, and public services, each warrants a full chapter in the revised Cohen. The next Cohen revision will see even more substantial changes as a new tapestry is rewoven. This is a task for each new generation.[9]

As to the specifics of the immediate future: I am not so good with the crystal ball. In the early 1960s I wrote with great assurance that the United States would never become involved in a ground war in Southeast Asia. Nonetheless, I will take a leap and suggest some ideas I believe crucial to the future of Indian law over the next generations.

There is no question that over the next decades Indian law will be increasingly more professional and increasingly in the hands of Indian peoples. This new generation of Indian lawyers is already at work within and outside the bureaucracy. Some law firms are coming to specialize in Indian law and are thus better able to keep abreast of current legal developments and to bring truly sophisticated resources to the aid of Indian peoples. More and more schools are adding Indian law to their curriculum. Furthermore, there is a body of legal literature including law journals, Web sites, indexes, and reporters devoted to Indian law. Also, there is our public-interest Indian law firm—the Native American Rights Fund; a current Indian law library center—the National Indian Law Library; Indian law organizations at university-based centers such as the Oklahoma City University Indian Legal Resources Center and private non-profits like the Institute for the Development of Indian Law, the American Indian Law Center, and the Indian Lawyers Training Program; the Indian Law Scholarship Program; the Indian Bar Association.

This growing professionalism brings increased responsibility and accountability to Indian law and Indian lawyers. For example, if Indian tribal courts are to function efficiently and be taken seriously, they must be self-policing—ready to guarantee the very highest standards of justice for their own citizens. Indian family and tribal nepotism cannot govern Indian law as it has too often governed in the past. Some sort of tribally originated protection of rights is needed so that Indian lawyers and judges in the tribal setting can make decisions involving tribal government and tribal officials without fear of removal or political interference. Rights, after all, bring with them responsibilities. And we do believe that there is something finer, better—more spiritual, if you will allow me—about Indian ways. Now is the time to prove it!

If Indian law is to prevail, Indian law must be worthy of prevailing, and that requires hard work and systematic effort. For a generation, Indian lawyers have enjoyed the luxury of being the performing exotic, the sequin sparkling for white audiences. In the next generation, traveling to conferences and debating Indian legal issues will not be enough without long hours in the library and at the typewriter or word processor. Long days of hard, nitty-gritty real lawyer work are ahead.

Indians have held out the promise; now we have to make it work. Often, it is easier to talk with other lawyers than to work with the Indian people who need us and our services. For they, too often, are not in three-piece suits or even well-designed ribbon shirts; they may be poorly educated—sometimes smelly, dirty, drunk, and drug-addicted. These are among the people for whom we have proclaimed the need for law, the people whom we profess to want to help. Sovereignty or no sovereignty, tribal Indians remain in the most desperate human need. And the kind of help they need doesn't always come from just the courthouse or the casebook.

In Indian law there must be a renewed recognition of the need for cooperation at all levels in meeting these human, social, and economic needs. Indian tribes are increasingly finding that litigation—a lawsuit—is not always the best answer. There are often positive alternatives such as agreements, compacts, and joint ventures. These work in areas as varied as economic development, taxation, treatment of substance abusers, water management, and criminal jurisdiction. Tribes, states, counties, and cities are learning that the costs of litigation may be too great. No one possesses enough time or resources to pridefully waste them, and that includes Indian peoples as well as state governments.

The fact that an Indian tribe may legally do something is not always a sound reason why they should. Flexing sovereignty muscles may cost more time and dollars than it is worth when in the criminal law area, for example, cross-deputization of tribal and state police can accomplish the very same thing. Furthermore, the "Indian-can-go-it-alone" philosophy doesn't always make sense when there are so many common Indian and non-Indian needs.

Let us also note that many of the best friends Indians have are non-Indians, often lawyers who have fought and won some of the great cases of the last decades. No matter how many Indian lawyers we graduate, we will continue to need the help of non-Indian attorneys—continue to need their friendship, knowledge, support, and most of all their keen and imaginative minds. If we had three or four times the number of Indian lawyers we now have, we would still not have enough for all the needs that will affect Indians over the next decades. This is particularly so as Indian Legal Services and the funding for its support comes under attack from congressional budget cutters.

As we look forward, we need to remember the lessons of the immediate past. Over the last decade, the pressure of breaking events has meant that too much of Indian law has been reactive rather than planned. Frequently, issues that were litigated were defensive, brought under the wrong circumstances and at the wrong place. Indian tribes went to the courts to put out fires; they were forced to the courthouse as a last-ditch effort. A coordinated strategy for law ought to be a part of the long-range planning of the Indian community. It is no secret that much of the early success of the African American civil rights movement came from a coordinated and closely planned strategy.

This is perhaps a good time to strike a recurring theme. Simply being an Indian, thinking great and good traditional spiritual thoughts, will not magically create an Indian attorney. Apprenticeships spent learning at the elbow— if not feet—of experienced masters of the profession is what is required. You've got to get into court: you can't dream away a stack of depositions. Indian clients need—as much if not more than others—lawyers who understand the economics of development, the intricacies of taxation, and the strategies of child and family law. Far more is needed than knowledge of the doctrine of tribal sovereignty.

Furthermore, lawyers for Indians must refuse to accept the conventional wisdom of the old legal doctrines, even when it comes from Felix Cohen. I can still remember young Geoffrey Standing Bear coming into my office in McFarlin Library at the University of Tulsa and saying to me: "How come you old guys haven't done something about tribal courts among the Five Civilized Tribes?" Of course, I was taken aback both about the "old guys" label and Geoff's lack of understanding of the "law" on tribal courts. "The Oklahoma Indian Welfare Act," he continued, "clearly authorizes Indian tribal courts and supersedes the Curtis Act attempt to close them down." As I said in defense of the "old guys", "we haven't been sitting here twiddling our thumbs." As I exhorted Geoff, "Each generation has a task, a challenge, and this one may be yours." And, sure enough, the courts agreed with the young guys; tribal courts have now returned to the Five Tribes because the "young guys" refused to accept the conventional legal wisdom.

Too often we have to reestablish the law, or even make new law. Indians and their lawyers must always be prepared to reexamine conventional assumptions and case interpretation. If there is one lesson of the last generation, it is that creativity and originality, combined with well-based historical research, provides the ammunition to force a reevaluation of the law. When I was teaching at the University of Wisconsin, we witnessed this rethinking in fishing rights. Nationally, we are currently seeing it on the reburial and repatriation question. Alaska and Hawaii's Native people are both beginning to test new ways to look at these principles in the context of their unique circumstances.

There are a number of settings, tribal and personal, in which the legal dimension of the Indian problem will certainly be present over the coming years. The surging legal activism of American Indians is not indicative of new problems, but a belated recognition of the legal dimension of age-old problems. Significant policy considerations with far-reaching legal implications are now being raised outside the litigation process, within the bureaucracy of the Indian administration or before congressional committees. Note the expanded powers given to tribes under the recently enacted "compacting" provisions of the Indian Self-Governance Act and the opportunities for economic development through revenue bonds and borrowing. Therefore, it would be a mistake to think that all of the most important legal issues will be raised in the courts. In fact, many of the truly serious legal and policy questions are faced by Indian leaders while guiding legislative and administrative decision making. It may not be too much of an exaggeration to say that what happens over the water cooler at the Aberdeen Area Office of the BIA may impact more on the life of Indian people than a decision of the United States Supreme Court.

A shift from the courtroom to the boardroom is also underway. Indian lawyers are becoming a significant part of a business development and economic expansion movement—and as part of teams that include bankers, economists, and tribal leaders. Over the coming decades, Indian legal advisors who do not understand corporate mergers, international taxation and business regulation, the bond and securities markets, and banking regulation will be outdated in the new fast-moving world of tribal economic independence and entrepreneurship.

In conclusion, I would like to preview what I suspect will be at the heart of future American Indian policy. Listed below are issues, settings, and circumstances that coming generations of lawyers will be called upon to address.

1. Internal or domestic tribal law will be increasingly more significant. For example, the tribe's need to zone and regulate environmental and economic questions will be necessary in preserving and protecting Indian life and lands. Gambling and bingo regulation will continue to test Indian tribal law, just as it tests state and federal law. Tribal codes and ordinances will require great attention and scrutiny. Substantially more legal infrastructure must be drafted, debated, and enacted on issues as technical as bills and notes and as broad as cultural preservation.

2. The urban Indian and the problems in the cities will require increased

time and resources, particularly with regard to claims for social services and in efforts to create new forums of tribal relations, service delivery systems, and medical, educational, and technical training opportunities. The Indian Child Welfare Act and the needs of the changing family, along with delivery of health care, remain central issues of Indian law and policy.

3. The vast body of Indian economic and natural resources, from fishing and hunting to water and minerals, will inevitably create new demands on Indian people, their lands, and their lawyers. Cooperation—co-management and co-development—with private developers, state agencies, private corporations, and individual citizens will hold the key to the role of the law in promoting tribal economic self-sufficiency. Sophisticated financing and sound entrepreneurial leadership must be produced. Tribes can expect new and imaginative efforts at both the state and federal levels to undermine historic legal rights and to gain access to these resources for non-Indian interests.

4. There are many unresolved land issues, including the question of interest on awards and the recognition of aboriginal rights, as well as simple leasing and management questions. Claims for land as well as damages will become crucial, particularly when addressed in Alaska and Hawaii. Protection of the lands of the allottees of the Five Tribes in eastern Oklahoma still needs to be removed from the state's district-court system. Furthermore, the trust status of Indian lands remains a target for anti-Indian interests.

5. New thrusts in the area of international law will raise issues of the relationship of Indian tribes to other native or indigenous peoples throughout the world, particularly in the context of their relationship with international organizations, treaties, and human rights. The international aspects of Indian law, especially in trade regulation, taxation, and economic expansion, are sure to be more central. Transfer of a number of Indian questions back to the State Department is being urged by a number of tribes.

6. Legal action will involve more legislation and administrative rulemaking. Indian lawyers will find themselves in the conference room more and in the courthouse less. More state and federal administrative agencies, many beyond the BIA and the Department of Interior, are destined to play larger roles in resolving Indian questions. Agency and commission relationships should be as crucial as the congressional. Despite the best long-range planning, there will always be the unexpected crisis that looms on the horizon, such as the Indian Death Penalty Act, taxation of gaming income, abolition of Indian legal services, elimination of the Indian functions of the Public Health Service, or elimination of the Bureau's authority to take historic tribal lands back into trust.

7. A number of Indian lawyers will have opportunities to work for Indian in-

terests—and their own—beyond the reservation and the Washington bureaucracy, in large corporate offices, communication conglomerates, universities,
oil companies, and the great Wall Street, Phoenix, Boston, and Washington
law firms. They will help bring new perspectives to the decision making of
America's ruling elite, and hopefully bring understanding of those perspectives
back into the more traditional practice of Indian law and to tribal leadership.

8. More and more—over the next decades—the BIA will be called to account
for failures as trustee to protect Indian tribes in negotiations of leases and
husbanding of resources. In the *Austin Walker* case, for example, a 600,000-
dollar judgment was entered against the Office of the Regional Solicitor in the
Department of Interior for malpractice on behalf of a Creek allottee. Tribes
will be called upon to balance and offset the declining role of the federal
bureaucracy, especially the substantial decline in budgeted funds. Numbers of
law suits are being filed to call for accountability on topics as diverse as the
individual trust accounts of Indian people and the collective interests of bands
of black freedmen, both mixed-bloods and former slaves.

9. There will be more tribal self-reliance and direct action as tribes discover
that programs they have contracted to perform under the old Indian Self-
Determination Act were underfunded and over-regulated even at the time of
transfer. More and more tribes will compact for more and more services under
the new self-governance regulations. So tribes, of necessity, will become more
aggressively independent in economic and legal matters. The day-to-day operation of tribal legal functions will become more significant as social programs
come to rest more heavily on Indian tribal groups and upon tribal resources.

10. Those significant and symbolic issues of patrimony—the return of skeletal remains and artifacts, the creation of the new national museum—will loom
even larger because they draw together a surging nationalistic spirit of Native
peoples. Tribes must begin the process of adopting and enforcing their own
regulations in these areas. Substantial victories must be taken beyond the
symbolic to actual resolution.

11. (And finally) one thing has not changed and is not likely to change for the
coming generations. Those seeking the survival of Native Americans and their
tribal governments must be ever watchful. One never knows from which
direction the next assault will come—be it a federal appeals tribunal to super-
vise tribal courts; a state role in regulating gaming; an Indian death-penalty act;
a restriction on tribal rights to take their former lands in trust. My brother, an
expert on "G.I. Rhetoric," used to quote General Patton to express the danger
of unexpected assaults. I'll clean Patton up a bit—it went something like this:
"If you ever shut your eyes, ever go to sleep, then the enemy will sneak up

behind you and hit you over the head with a sack of [high grade equine manure]."

In conclusion, I suspect the days of the great old Indian sport of BIA bashing may be drawing to a close. In fact, if many in Congress have their way the Bureau may become a ghost agency. Indian people are increasingly being summoned to testify before the Congress and asked what they think ought to be done. Tribes are increasingly represented by delegates and ambassadors in Washington and are a part of the action inside the beltway. Even more tribes need such help, support, and presence—remembering it is true that the price of liberty is eternal vigilance. The time has now come when we have to do more than point our fingers and shake our fists. And this is where the Indian lawyer worth her salt must be prepared to step forward, climb out on the limb, and make that educated and informed, yet intuitive leap of faith and recommend what ought to be done and then go ahead and do it. And this must be done without losing track with tribal people far from the glory and glamour of the Potomac Indian.

The challenges and opportunities of the generations are great. What Indian lawyers convinced legislators and judges that sovereign Indian tribes and competent Indian people were capable of doing must now be done. We are at the proof of the legal pudding stage. The rhetoric of the courtroom and the legislative hall must now be actualized. That is the challenge for all our generations—and a worthy one, indeed. This historic challenge neither begins nor ends with us; the challenge is part of T. C. Cannon's ribbonlike flow that is our Native American heritage.

I would like to close on that challenge. If there is a lesson, a negative one, in George Longfish's *You Can't Rollerskate in a Buffalo Herd Even If You Have All the Medicine*, there is a positive lesson in another of his paintings. *Spirit Guide/Spirit Healer* (1983) is about the survival of traditional values, of the perplexities of application of modern technology to universal human needs.[10] Longfish tells us that strength comes from being historically rooted. Our direction through the modern maze must come from the ancient, from the *Spirit Guide/Spirit Healer*. And that, I believe, is the common lesson for all the generations. Our tasks may vary, but our goals must remain the same. After all, who but one of D. H. Lawrence's disintegrated psyches would want to rollerskate in a buffalo herd, anyway?

CHAPTER FOUR

BEYOND THE ETHNIC UMBRELLA
AND THE BLUE DEER
Some Thoughts for Collectors of Native Painting and Sculpture

Over many decades the art world has vigorously debated the "Indianness" of Native American painting and sculpture. In art, as in life, few controversies are really new. The debate over Native American artistic images mirrors the nineteenth-century quest for ethnic, racial, and national qualities in European and American painting. In 1875 a *Scribner's* critic argued that "an American, an Englishman, a Dutchman, an Italian, and a Frenchman, called upon to plant an umbrella, one after another, in the same spot, and paint the same scene, will produce pictures so different from each other, in handling and effect, as to warrant their being presented and preserved in a group upon the same wall."[1]

Somehow, today this historic search for national or racial artistic schools seems outdated, quaintly Victorian. Yet it is at the heart of a continuing Indian art controversy. The debaters ask: Is there an Indian art style? Is Indian painting all painting by any Indian? Does Indian painting require an Indian theme? In short, is the Indian umbrella a preordained form in the Indian mind? We too could assemble a wall of artistic umbrellas all created by Native Americans. How, for example, would one compare the ethnicity of the nineteenth-century Cheyenne artist Buffalo Meat, in his ledger book–style painting *Indian with Horse*, with the ethnicity of T. C. Cannon, in his lithograph *Indian Princess Waiting for the Bus in Anadarko*? Both carry the ubiquitous umbrella. Would Fritz Scholder's *Indians with Umbrellas* be more or less truly Indian than Dorothy Trujillo's ceramic figure *Pueblo Potter with Umbrella on Market Day*?[2]

"Art," Georges Braque proclaimed, "is meant to disturb." And much that is happening in contemporary Indian painting and sculpture is disturbing. Many important questions in the Indian-painting debate are not easily answered.

The conscientious collector seeks self-education to enhance both appreciation and understanding. Knowledge and appreciation is worth the collector's quest, for this is the way to informed connoisseurship.

The great American painters of the nineteenth century, when asked how to understand and identify "good painting," told their patrons to look and to look and to look again. One understands and appreciates art by seeing art—both the good and the bad. Art is intended to be experienced emotionally as well as intellectually. This is as true of a modern Native American abstraction as it was of an Eakins or Chase portrait. The eyes are informed by the mind and heart; the serious student of Indian painting and sculpture wants to know, to see, and to feel. We hope to know what the artist is trying to achieve. Thus, we need to be aware of the Indian artistic tradition and the cultural and religious roles that art plays in tribal life. Further, we must understand how the Indian has interacted with white culture. As the Indian dips into the so-called mainstream, the broader cultural currents of the Anglo artistic tradition become increasingly strong. If we are to regard Indian painting as more than an ethnographic curiosity, then we must look for more than an Indian subject and a flat, two-dimensional style.

One of the threshold difficulties in understanding Indian painting and sculpture is that contemporary Native painting is lumped with all other Indian art. Navajo rugs and Sioux beaded saddles and Salish horn spoons are compared with books of Kiowa ledger paintings and Hopi watercolors of Kachina dancers and Creek abstract oils of desert landscapes. It is thus more difficult to make informed, comparative judgments about Indian painting and sculpture. It is a little like evaluating all European artistic achievement by looking collectively at silver spoons, carved monastery doors, illuminated manuscripts, and the paintings of Claude Monet. Furthermore, there were as many as two thousand historic North American Indian tribes, bands, and village groups with more than two hundred languages. Utilitarian, sacred, and ornamental objects come together in our minds under the heading "Indian Art." All have influenced, in some way or other, contemporary Native painting and sculpture. But painting and sculpture must be evaluated as painting and sculpture if we are to understand them and their role in the broader artistic tradition.

Further analytical refinement is needed even when painting and sculpture are viewed in isolation from other Native arts. In this house are many artistic mansions. There is no single Indian painting style. Native artists continue to draw in the old hide-ledger-book styles, to paint in the studio traditional mode, to follow trends as divergent as photo realism and abstract expressionism. Almost every school of contemporary artistic expression has an Indian exponent. Beyond that are the Indian stylistic refinements and streaks of individual genius that make Indians leaders whose styles are followed, in turn, by non-Indians. One cannot make a single generalization describing all of contemporary Indian painting and sculpture. Indian artists are following too many roads.

To understand what is happening in Native American arts requires visiting tribal villages and reservations, museums, and galleries to look and to look and to look. A supplement, but not a substitute, for visiting museums is the glorious body of reproductions and books of reproductions of American Indian painting, which can provide the serious student with the richness of major public and private collections.

Art on museum walls and in the pages of books is different from art in a living culture. By a stroke of luck we have a chance to see the role that art played in Indian life captured in a remarkable early film made by Edward S. Curtis in 1914. This pioneer quasi-documentary, originally released as *In the Land of the Headhunters*, now known as *In the Land of the War Canoes*, was the first full-length motion picture about an aboriginal North American society. While the plot is melodramatic, the dances are unmistakably real. When Thunderbird and Grizzly Bear dance, the soul of the animal awakens. There is instant understanding of a vitality we have previously only been told about or sensed intellectually. The dancer is not portraying Grizzly Bear; the dancer *is* Grizzly Bear. Bill Holm and George Irving Quimby produced and restored the film for a release with the addition of musical backgrounds.[3] One of the best ways to begin to understand this aspect of Indian art and life is to see Indian ceremonials. One can then begin to appreciate how central Indian art is to Indian life.

In the disjointed Indian-art debates, a number of issues have become confused. Whether or not an Indian is an Indian artist when he paints an abstracted umbrella is a different issue from how successfully the Indian artist paints that abstracted umbrella. Some patrons who dislike modernism have decided that only what existed in Indian culture before a preordained time such as the beginning of the twentieth century, when Curtis was staging his photographs or in the time of the Studio in Santa Fe before the Second World War, is an appropriately Indian art form. These patrons search for modifications of historic aspects of the Indian art with which they are comfortable. Seizing on bits and pieces of the whole artistic tradition, they have created canons, rules, and tenets for Indian painting. For example, one group of critics demanded no modeling, perspective, or background under their guidelines. Others demand "artistic freedom" for Indian painters to explore styles beyond the sanctioned tradition. These patrons often extravagantly praise experimentation simply because it is a deviation from the prewar Indian artistic norm.

Freedom and quality are often confused by both sides in the debate. It is possible to believe that personal freedom is the essence of art and that Indian painters ought to explore new artistic avenues, but also to believe that a part of what is being created may be aesthetically ineffectual. There can be mediocre cubist or surrealist Indian painters, just as there can be terrible and trite traditionalists. Furthermore, Indian traditionalism, revived and revitalized, may be remarkably alive, while much that is current in European and American art may be more moribund.

Students of the history of modernism are familiar with the depth of twentieth-century artists' interest in primitivism. For example, the influences of works like African and American Indian masks or Navajo sand painting can be seen in contemporary painters and sculptors from Picasso to Moore to Pollock. It is ironic that the moderns forced us to understand the sophistication of the primitive and to appreciate differing levels of reality.

As Native American painters are increasingly influenced by modern non-Indian painters who were in turn influenced by the primitive, we have a classic example of double cross-fertilization. It is like a mirror reflecting back upon a mirror. The image goes on and on and on. The contemporary Indian mirrors the cubist, who mirrors the carver of primitive masks, who mirrors the Native world view. Thus the modern Indian artist lives in a house of mirrors. He stands face to face with both ethnic and artistic images. For example, white society has created an image of the Indian, a racial stereotype that is but a mirror of the problems of white society itself. Likewise, there is the Indian society's own image of itself and of white society. Images endlessly reflect back into themselves.

Patrons of Native American art often view Indian painting as an evolutionary process; they see a family tree that runs from primitive to modern, from traditional to abstract. No doubt there is remarkable continuity in theme and style. But the process comes full circle, returning to many of the ancient forms and ideas. The ancestral painter of the abstracted parrot or turkey on a Mimbres pot or the artist who drew the hands on a Hopi Sikyatki bowl was doing exactly what the Hopi Choctaw painter Linda Lomahaftewa is doing in her paintings *Night Parrot #2* and *Cosmic Hands*.[4] The primitive and the modern are parts of the same artistic tradition. While Indian art has multiple artists and thereby multiple intentions, the Indian cultural worldview is the essence of Native American painting, whether the style is traditionalism or individualism. All speak to an Indian experience in an Indian idiom.

The ledger-book creator of battlefield Indian riders was not trying to reproduce the Battle of Little Bighorn photographically. These artists are "reductionists," painting symbols that go to the essence of being. Indian art may seem clumsy and ineffectual if the viewer believes the Native artist is trying to paint a real horse in the style of a European salon painter. Indian art becomes highly sophisticated abstraction when the viewer understands why the painter draws transparent horses stacked horse upon horse. It is not childish gibberish, but a language of philosophical metaphor whereby the artist communicates at a different level of reality. The work of art explains itself to those who understand the symbols and the worldview they embody. An increasingly secular Western society whose art is a nihilistic statement of the degeneration of values has difficulty understanding the art of a deeply religious society whose art is an affirmation of an ongoing and shared consensus of values.

Indian art has moved from the anonymous artist to the identified painter, carver, potter, and weaver. There has naturally been an increased emphasis upon personal achievement and the life, career, and artistic motivation of the individual artist. The Indian's vision, what the artist thinks he is doing, is crucial to an understanding and appreciation of Indian painting.

Art must be understood in a cultural context. We know that one both naturally absorbs and is formally taught the values and unstated assumptions of the culture in which she grows up. For the American Indian, many values are deeply religious and tied to mystical experiences. In Western culture a personal symbol or vision or song seems on the surface to have less value as property than such incorporeal assets have in Indian culture. Yet in non-Indian society Coca Cola fights to preserve a trademark, radio stations pay royalties when they play "Happy Birthday," and Disney sues at the hint of misuse of Mickey and Donald. One who understands the mystical and spiritual nature of Indian society sees Indian art more clearly. Wintu artist Frank LaPeña's *Deer Rattle—Deer Dancer* and Creek artist Acee Blue Eagle's *The Deer Spirit* impart a different vision to an Indian who knows the role of ghosts from that imparted to someone with a literalistic or mathematical outlook. Societies, of course, borrow symbols, and some symbols become almost universal—as in Woody Big Bow's traditional portrait of an Indian woman, whose middle finger is extended in the air to reflect displeasure.

Many of the jokes of a culture are difficult to transfer or translate. Despite white stereotypes of stoic and frozen-faced Indians, humor is at the heart of much Indian life, culture, and art. In part, that is because the only way to survive in the face of much of what white society has done to the Indian is to laugh—both at the white man and at the bitter irony of one's own plight. Early Northwest Coast carvers with their wonderfully pompous argillite sculptures of white sailors and ship captains were doing what Fritz Scholder, Bob Haozous, T. C. Cannon, and Grey Cohoe have done. But Indian humor in art is not simply defensive; Indian art is more than a combat force. There has been some movement away from the painter's openly political posturing of the 1960s and early 1970s. Today the Indian's polemical statements are more deeply integrated into the creative process and the finished work. The colors and shadows of Grey Cohoe's widely reproduced *Tocito Waits for Boarding School Bus* speak more eloquently of the Indian educational experience than slogan-painted posters and drawings. Coyote in Harry Fonseca's world is a mirror in which the painter gives the trickster animal human frailty. Thus the Indian artist does what the Indian storyteller has always done: he makes us laugh at ourselves.

It is impossible to understand painting and sculpture without a broader understanding of the imagery of all native arts and crafts. Unfortunately, there is no published iconography for designs and themes in Indian painting. Discussions of motifs from pottery, masks, basketry, Kachina, jewelry, weaving, and other arts are basic to easel art and sculpture. For comparative purposes, the works of the non-Indian painters of Indians and Indian life must also be studied. Both the American and the European traditions are rich with these images.

Indian art must become the subject of thoughtful study of individuals of all perspectives. Serious collecting requires serious thought and inquiry—even serious scholarship. No longer should Indian painting and sculpture be considered in isolation, classed alternatively as ethnography or artifact or fine art or tourist curio. Only when a new perspective has been established can we begin to understand the universal aspects of Indian art. Only then will we begin to appreciate the perspectives of folk art, craft art, primitive art, fine art, erotic art, ethnic art, and protest art that are reflected in Indian painting and sculpture. Only then will we understand the divergent influences of historical events and artistic developments. Only then will we be able to relate the spiritual dimension of Indian art to broader goals and human values. Only then will Native artists themselves be recognized as true national treasures.

The Indian artist is caught today in a debate over the ethnicity of his umbrella. The dilemma of the Indian painter is sharply focused in many of the works of the late Kiowa-Caddo artist T. C. Cannon. The most vivid of these is his famous *Collector #5*, sometimes known as *Osage with Van Gogh*. As a painting, a poster, and a woodcut, *Collector #5* has taken on artistic significance in the Indian-art debate. Abstract issues are personified by this finely dressed Osage sitting in his wicker chair between a Navajo rug and Van Gogh's *Wheatfield*. The worlds of mainstream and Indian art are here represented. In a sense, this is a modern version of Wohow's ledger drawing from Fort Marion, in which a Kiowa warrior stands symbolically posed between a buffalo and a cow, between the hunt and the farm. As Karen Peterson notes in describing

Wohow's masterpiece, "The Indian stands between two cultures."[5] Cannon is saying that the modern Indian makes his own culture and his own art, drawing from both worlds. The confident and smiling Osage proclaims that whatever he makes or does is uniquely and appropriately Indian.

Cannon's paintings tell us that to be a Native American is bitter as well as sweet medicine. To be an artist in any society is to be, in Thomas Wolfe's words, "life's hungry man." To be an Indian artist in white society is to be doubly cursed and twice blessed, to live in an ethnic house of mirrors. As in a carnival house, the mirrors reflect and refract, distort and deflect. The artist sees objects that endlessly reflect back into themselves. Each of us, W. H. Auden wrote, carries a mirror through life. In this mirror, Shaw observed, we see our faces; in art we see mirrored our souls. Living in a house of mirrors is a curse; creating in a house of mirrors may be a blessing. In the Indian's house of mirrors, the observant Native American artist may see around and through, glimpsing beyond the glittering surfaces and back into the deep reaches of the soul.

Let us look at one final Indian umbrella. In T. C. Cannon's painting *Grandmother Gestating Father and the Washita River Runs Ribbon-Like*, the artist portrays an obviously pregnant Indian woman walking along a narrow stream. The madonna's face is partly hidden under the shadow of her red umbrella, but she looks out directly into the world. This madonna speaks of the strength and resilience of Native American life and the survival of the Indian spirit.[6]

Looking at Native American easel art across generations, the sense of unity is great. The number of factors drawing the generations of twentieth-century painters together is far greater than those separating them. Nonetheless, postwar modern Indian painting is marked both by great continuity and by great change. The single greatest factor spanning the fifty years from 1945 to 1995 is the emerging depth and diversity of Native American easel art. During this half-century any pretense of a single, unified, Indian painting style completely disappeared. If, at the beginning of the postwar period, it was possible to identify Indian painting as flat, nonmolded watercolor records of tribal legend, history, and custom, by the end of the period it would be impossible to catalogue Indian easel art styles without listing a full range of diverse multi-original and multimedia styles.

The title of an historic panel on Indian art accurately summarized this contemporary diversity as "Indian painting from ledger to laser art." Today more Indians are painting in more styles with more success than at any other time in the history of Indian painting. There are traditionalists who continue to paint in the Studio or Plains style, as well as neo-traditional ledger-style painters and videotape event and performance artists; there are abstract illusionists and there are creators of found-object collages; there are lithographers, engravers, and photographers. All are Indian but not all are creating works that are identifiably Indian in subject matter, a fact that continues to disturb some patrons and even a few critics of Indian art.

The world of contemporary Indian painting is in many ways a reflection of the world of the American Indian in general and the non-Indian art world and market in particular. The fifty years since the end of World War II has produced a significant number of developments. For example, Indian artists are creating for a broader market, working in multi-originals such as lithographs, engravings, woodcuts, and serigraphs. On the whole, large numbers of Indian painters tend to be professional artists with fine art school training and a sophisticated understanding of both art history and technique. These Indian artists are self-confident and have broad and cosmopolitan experiences, including considerable interaction among themselves and with sophisticated support systems and worldwide networks. A growing number have income-producing careers associated with universities, museums, cultural organizations, and educational programs. Others have developed strong gallery or patron associations, and most earn their daily bread from art. The present generation of Indian artists tend to be more involved in organizing their own exhibitions and in the marketing and critical evaluation of Indian art. All of these trends are apparent across the postwar generations. They have considerable intergenerational contact and there are a number of multi-generational artistic families, such as the Kaboties, the Gormans, Peña-Herrera, Houser-Hoazous, and Velarde-Hardin. Contemporary Indian painters of the postwar era are the beneficiaries (or targets) of a growing body of critical studies and of a variety of museum and institutional support, ranging from the pioneering Rockefeller Project at the University of Arizona to mainstream critiques in the *New York Times* and the *Washington Post*.

Emerging at the apex of contemporary Indian art is sculpture, particularly the unique wood sculpture of Apache Allan Houser, Cheyenne Dick West, and Cherokee Willard Stone. Looking at wood, these artists have the eye of the Indian and the soul of a creator. To some people a tree is only so many broad feet of timber, graded lumber stacked and ready for sale. When an Indian sees a cedar tree, he may see a mystical relationship of man and nature, a story coming from the grain of the uncut piece of walnut or maple.

A classic example of contemporary Native American wood sculpture is Dick West's *Cheyenne Wolf Warrior*. The Indian has on his face the defiant expression of the wolf whose skin he wears as a part of the costume of the Cheyenne Soldier Society. The head of the wolf hanging from his chest conveys the knowledge that the warrior has taken the power and spirit of the animal into his heart. One of Willard Stone's works, which he considers his finest, is *Young Rabbithawk*. Here, the mystical relationship between Stone, the Cherokee Indian artist, and the creatures of nature are revealed. The wood is smooth, the natural formations of the grain in the tree make the bird's feathers, his face, and the heart on his chest. In turn, Stone says, *Young Rabbithawk* symbolizes the Cherokee Indian as he looks out on the modern world. Similarly, Houser's *Camp Crier* uses angles in a small chunk of walnut to portray not only the strength but even the functionality of the private tribal leader who daily spread the news and created the unity of the village.

In assessing postwar trends in present-day Indian easel art, a number of changes are apparent. The single greatest is the diversity of media. Today, drawings (pastel, pencil, and pen) are important to the Indian artist and the Indian art world. Through multi-originals, particularly lithographs, Indian artists have expanded the market for Native art and added a new dimension to the artistic mastery. Unfortunately, low-quality offset prints of original Indian paintings have become an overpriced staple of this market. Intended to create an investment opportunity, these color prints in editions as large as a thousand are generally financial as well as artistic failures. Indian painters have generally shifted emphasis away from the precise historical ethnographic recording of legends and events such as dances, hunts, and ceremonials. Today, artists more frequently address the spirit, the symbols, or values of Indianness—the so-called spirituality. This change may be inevitable because earlier generations of artists were capturing their own historic firsthand experiences, which are beyond recall for the present generation. The question of the essential spirit of Indianness is a more relevant one for Native Americans living and working and interacting in an increasingly white-dominated urban world.

The continuity of iconography is clear, but Indian art has recently focused on a number of new subjects not widely used by earlier Native American painters. These include landscapes, portraits, and both male and female nudes, some with an eroticism reflective of Waldo Mootzka's deco-inspired corn fertility series from the thirties. Indian life has always been rich in humor, and the ironic dimension of the modern Indian's world is increasingly used by artists like Rick Danay for work like his *Mohawk Headdress*, a painted construction worker's hard hat; Bob Haozous's wonderful drawing of the pretentiousness of the New Mexico art community in *Taos Lady*; or Fritz Scholder's *Super Indian with Coors* or *Buffalo Dancer with Strawberry Ice Cream Cone*.

There is both a blurring of regional styles and an affirmation of differences among the Woodland, Southwest, or Northwest tribes in the emergence of a neo-traditional style that pays homage to older painters such as the nineteenth-century ledger artists. A group of Kiowas working through the Jacobson Center in Norman, Oklahoma, have exhibited together and created an informal "New Kiowa Movement" in much the way the Hopi cooperative Artists Hopid did beginning in 1973. Other significant cross-influences include the renewed borrowing of bead, pottery, rug, and basket designs in easel art.

Despite such change, much of the critical literature of modern Indian art continues to focus upon a fundamental question of definition, of Indianness, and of the symbols of and for Native people. Ironically, the major figure in this historic struggle between the traditional and the modern over an Indian style and subject matter has been the little-painted deer. Innocent-eyed creatures, they stare out in cervine splendor, peering from hundreds (perhaps thousands) of American Indian paintings. The deer, more than the buffalo or the bear or even the eagle, stand for what proponents of modernism in Indian painting regard as the curio, tourist, colorist, colonial, white-dictated "Bambi School" of Native American art.

If art is about symbols and symbolism, then the blue deer and her brother and sister deer have come, in the popular mind, to stand for the worst sort of trite commercialism in traditional Indian painting. And yet the painted deer could just as easily represent the achievement of this depth and diversity in contemporary American Indian painting and sculpture. In fact, the last one hundred years of the paintings of deerlike creatures demonstrates that even from the very beginning, the more creative Indian artists have continually brought new and fresh insights into the iconography of and about Native peoples. The deer, mistakenly seen as a symbol of the static, can be as easily seen as a figure representing both continuity and change, a symbol joining together historic and contemporary Indian painting and painters.

The half-century since the end of the Second World War has been both a trying and triumphant time for the Native painter. By the end of the 1960s or the beginning of the 1970s, Indian artists of all the postwar generations loudly complained of the absurd practice of critics and potential patrons searching the paintings of native artists for Indian signs such as a deer or a bear, a buffalo, a tipi, or an arrow. This attitude too often produced an automatic rejection from competitions and galleries of paintings that did not adequately demonstrate "Indianness" by the use of appropriate symbols such as the deer. On the other hand, strong proponents of modernism might just as arbitrarily reject paintings that did incorporate such symbolism, even when the symbolism was imaginatively and creatively evoked. Indian artists further argued that in this atmosphere their ability to show and to sell depended upon the way others defined their painterly obligations. They found many critics and collectors condemning as non-Indian the artist who did not paint in a preconceived orthodox style such as the flat, traditional watercolor. And fine traditional

Native artists were equally frustrated by the rejection of their work as outdated tourist art. Fortunately, for artists of the 1990s this battle has become largely history.

The most famous response to what has been called "the Indian art witch hunt" is contained in a letter from the Sioux painter Oscar Howe to Philbrook Museum Indian Art Curator Jeannie Snodgrass King after one of his cubist works had been rejected by a juror as "non-Indian." Howe observes:

> There is much more to Indian Art, than pretty, stylized pictures. There was also power and strength and individualism (emotional and intellectual insight) in the old Indian paintings. Every bit in my paintings is a true studied fact of Indian paintings. Are we to be held back forever with one phase of Indian painting, with no right for individualism, dictated to as the Indian always has been, put on reservations and treated like a child, and only the White Man knows what is best for him? Now, even in Art, "You little child do what we think is best for you, nothing different." Well, I am not going to stand for it. Indian Art can compete with any Art in the world, but not as a suppressed Art.
>
> I see so much of the mismanagement and treatment of my people. It makes me cry inside to look at these poor people. My father died there about three years ago in a little shack, my two brothers still living there in shacks, never enough to eat, never enough clothing, treated as second class citizens. This is one of the reasons I have tried to keep the fine ways and culture of my forefathers alive. But one could easily turn to become a social protest painter. I only hope the Art World will not be one more contributor to holding us in chains.[7]

Much of this historic controversy surrounding the little blue deer grows from a tendency to confuse iconography and style. Even to this day, in much of the public mind the subject matter of Indian painting is indistinguishable from the technique of the painter. In Indian painting, almost as much as in dance, there is an unwillingness or inability to separate the painter from the painting, to differentiate the "Indianness" of the subject matter from either the quality of the painting or the painter. Thus, there survived in the period after World War II an orthodoxy of Native American painting, a preconceived notion of topics and symbols as well as styles considered acceptable for Indian paintings. Much of the history of Indian painting over the past half-century has been about shaking off this orthodoxy. In more recent years the focus has shifted to the ethnic identity or tribal enrollment of artists.

The iconographic orthodoxy of Indian painting produced a dilemma for the innovative Native American painter seeking to move in what in the late fifties and early sixties was called "new directions" of Indian painting. These new directions were a focus of the Rockefeller Workshops at the University of Arizona and the Institute of American Indian Arts in Santa Fe, which grew out of those workshops. The dilemma operated this way. The painter who was an Indian was denied his or her Indianness if one of the accepted symbols was not used in his or her work, while at the same time the painter who was an Indian might alternatively be condemned as trite and repetitive if one of the symbols were employed. The question for the artist became: What does a Native American painter do when he or she wants to say something about the deer or the deer people or the deer spirit? Is the work only "Bambi art?" Can it be more? Or, on the other hand, what is to be the fate of the American Indian painter who finds all of this about deer or buffalo to be a great bore unrelated to his or her present-day life as an Indian and wants to paint about law school or video arcades or motorcycle symbols or bars and drunks?

A look at several paintings of deer by Indian artists illustrates the diversity possible in the treatment of this single symbolic figure. What is important in these paintings is not that each artist painted this animal but that each, in painting the animal, conveyed so much that was unique and original and that each deer, rather than being static and clichéd, is, in a peculiarly personal way, an innovative and insightful artistic statement. More than half a century ago John Sloan, an early student of Indian painting, noted a particular metaphysical relationship in an early Pueblo deer-dance composition. Sloan felt that "when Awa Tsireh sits down to paint a leaping deer he remembers not only the way a deer looks leaping over a log but he feels himself leaping in the dance with antlers swaying on his forehead and two sticks braced in hands for forelegs."[8]

The deer paintings considered here cover a period of more than half a century, ranging from an intricate and stylized deer design by Richard Martinez drawn in the 1920s through a free-flowing monotype by Fritz Scholder from the 1980s. During these years, the deer (blue, red, pink, and otherwise) was painted thousands of times by hundreds of Indian artists, painted on shields and on pottery, on paper and on hide. Not all Indian deer paintings are going to be good; many are bad, really bad. The deer, like the oft-painted carp or cat of oriental art, deserves to be judged by the best and not the worst, not by the ordinary. After all, generations of Asian masters have drawn fine and delicate designs capturing swimming fish and mysterious felines, changing them almost imperceptibly, but refining and restating the symbol.

Anyone who carefully examines a wall of these deer paintings must conclude that Indian painting has changed both gradually and dramatically over the years. Cecil Dick's *Deer Hunt* suggests the influence of art deco; Gerald Nailor's

The Quiet Way conjures an Asian mood. Both Acee Blue Eagle's *The Deer Spirit* and Frank LaPeña's *Deer Rattle/Deer Dancer*, though executed in the radically different traditional and modern styles, suggest a common spirituality. It is fun to compare Velino Herrera's *Deer Dancers* with the dancing deer in Fritz Scholder's *Deer at Laguna*. And, of course, there is the highly stylized and typically classical deer of Ernest Lewis's *Just Passing Through*, which reminds us that Indian art is an art of thought which, even in the simplest of the so-called "Bambi paintings," asks difficult questions. What do the two deer prancing past the aspens know that we do not know about God's stewardship? About the bluebirds overhead? About the clouds in the sky?[9]

Let me conclude by saying that Indian painting and sculpture is one of the most exciting and dynamic art movements in the world. There is no finer nor more beautiful art being produced than the works of the Native American artist. One has the sense of something that is fresh and meaningful, even lasting, in the works of American Indian painters and sculptures. As Oscar Howe reminded us: "There is much more to Indian art, than pretty, stylized pictures." The true collector, the serious connoisseur, has the chance and the challenge, indeed the obligation, to discover what Howe identified as the "power and strength and individualism [and] emotional and intellectual insight."

CHAPTER FIVE

TO DO THE RIGHT THING
Reaffirming Indian Traditions of Justice Under Law

No people on the North American continent are more closely identified with law than the Cherokee. Even today, whenever issues of Indian law are joined in the courts, the early nineteenth-century Cherokee removal cases—*Cherokee Nation v. Georgia*[1] and *Worcester v. Georgia*[2]—are cited. When the story of the birth of tribal constitutionalism is documented, the Cherokees are listed as the first Indian tribe to adopt a written law and establish a formal constitution. The United States, on the occasion of the two-hundredth anniversary of the U.S. Constitution, acknowledged the contribution of the Iroquoian peoples, of whom the Cherokees are the southernmost tribe. The legal heritage of the wampums entrusted to the Keetoowah begins at the very beginning of life on this continent. It can be said, without equivocation, that the Cherokee are truly a people of law.

This morning with the rededication of the Cherokee National Capitol we are celebrating and reaffirming that tradition. I have taken the title "To Do the Right Thing" from an 1877 letter written by a Cherokee-speaking court officer of the Goingsnake District. The solicitor wrote to Chief Thompson: "I do not desire to keep the job just because of the salary. . . . It has become desirable to do the right thing."[3] This morning I want us to visit about doing the right thing.

From 1808 until 1898 the Cherokee tribe operated tribal courts based upon their own written laws, codes, and constitutions. Throughout the nineteenth century, outside observers who came into the nation chronicled the honesty and efficiency of the system. They also noted that support for Cherokee law was nearly universal among all tribal groups, from fullblood traditionalists to mixed-blood acculturationists. Since I have waived my usual speaking fee this morning, Chief Mankiller promised me I could plug one of my books. In *Fire and the Spirits*,[4] I recorded many details about the operation of the Cherokee legal system and provide a chronology of key dates and a summary of the early tribal laws. Relax, you are not going to be subjected to a law professor's Socratic cross-examination and case parsing. The story is there available for purchase in fine book stores everywhere. Suffice it to say, at the beginning of the nineteenth century, the Cherokees cast their fate into the mainstream of the American legal process. Few have done the process greater honor than the Cherokee.

In the struggle to retain their ancestral homes in Georgia in the 1830s, the Cherokee awaited the decision of Chief Justice John Marshall and the Supreme Court. The Marshall Court, in the famous *Worcester v. Georgia*,[5] supported the Cherokee cause and reaffirmed the Cherokee belief in the legal process. Then Jackson is purported to have issued his famous challenge to the judiciary— "Marshall has made his law, let him enforce it."[6] Marshall and the Cherokees had the law. Jackson had the troops.

With a Supreme Court decision in their favor, fifteen thousand Cherokees were driven by General Winfield Scott and his troops out of their beloved southern mountain homelands. Only eleven thousand finished the journey; four thousand died along the trek, which we know as the "Trail of Tears." This incident is germane to our activities this morning because it vividly illustrates the Indians' historic dilemma. As soon as a tribe adapted to new ways in an effort to survive, the United States, through force of arms or legislation, destroyed what the tribe had done. The pattern was repeated again and again.

At the close of the nineteenth century, the Cherokee and their brother and sister tribes, the Creeks, Chickasaws, Choctaws, and Seminoles, had developed legal systems more just and efficient than most states. They stood ready to accept the dream that their negotiations had held-out—admission to the Union as an Indian state. The Cherokees had moved to a truly well-run, almost a model, court process and now waited for the long-promised Indian State that would culminate their historic compromise. Instead, the United States Congress and the instrument of their creation, the Dawes Commission, divided tribal lands, abolished Indian courts, and attempted to end forever the governing powers of the Indian nations. The Cherokees and the other Civilized Tribes were forced to abandon their Indian State of Sequoyah and were involuntarily merged into the state of Oklahoma.

It is during this dark period that Redbird Smith, the visionary leader of the Keetoowah traditionalists, said: "My greatest ambition has always been to think right and do right. It is my belief that this is the fulfilling of the law of the Great Creator . . . I have always believed the Great Creator had a great design for my people, the Cherokees. I have been taught that from my childhood up and now in my mature manhood I recognize it as a great truth. Our forces have been dissipated by external forces, perhaps it has been just a training, but we must now get together . . . and render our contribution to mankind. We are endowed with intelligence, we are industrious, we are loyal, and we are spiritual but we are overlooking the particular Cherokee mission on earth—for no man nor race is endowed with these qualifications without a designed purpose. . . . Our pride in our ancestral heritage is our great incentive for handing something worthwhile to our posterity. It is this pride in ancestry that makes men strong and loyal for their principle in life."[7] Surely, it is so.

The rededication of this national capitol and the reopening of the courts, which we celebrate today, is but one small example of Redbird Smith's prophetic words and of the tribal quest "to think right and do right." The recent Cherokee legislative enactment requiring the teaching of tribal history for all national employees is an official recognition of Smith's conclusion that "our ancestral heritage is our great incentive for handing something worthwhile to our posterity."[8]

Nearly a century ago, it did not appear that law, much less the Cherokee Nation and its ancestral heritage, would endure for tribal posterity. In 1898, the clerk of the Cherokee Supreme Court, sitting in this capitol building here in Tahlequah, wrote the last entry on the ledger pages of the official record book: the end of the court session and the absence of the Cherokee tribal justices were duly noted. The Supreme Court record book for that final year opens with the federal orders closing Cherokee courts; then the pages are blank. Thus, in 1898 Cherokee courts closed and their formal use of the Cherokee written law summarily ended. Under federal law, Cherokee judges were no longer allowed to enforce their own tribal regulation; indeed, to have held court would have made the judges criminals.

We are here this morning to formally mark the end of that federal interdict and acknowledge the tribal rebirth of the Cherokee court system. I am deeply honored to have been asked to deliver this celebratory address, an address acknowledging the Cherokee historical tradition of government under law and anticipating the forthcoming achievements of new generations of Cherokee leadership and law. In preparation for this speech, I went to the archives of the Oklahoma Historical Society and once again examined the leather-bound volumes which are the official record of the seven Cherokee district courts and the Supreme Court of the Cherokee Nation. I reviewed the court volumes—district by district. It is an impressive judicial linage, a great ancestral heritage.

As I looked at the faded pages with the flourish of elaborate, handwritten nineteenth-century records of hearings and trials and appeals, I saw, in my mind's eye, that group of Cherokee deputies, in Washington, in January of 1809. And I heard, in the movie of my mind, Thomas Jefferson speaking to them about the introduction of what the president called "the regular administration of laws." Jefferson, author of the Declaration of Independence, spoke the following words to the assembled Cherokee delegation: "I sincerely wish you may succeed in your laudable endeavors to save . . . your nation, by adopting industrious occupations and government of regular laws."[9]

Less than ninety years later a new president and his federal marshals did not wish the Cherokee Nation well, indeed, they did not wish the Cherokees to continue what Jefferson had urged them to begin. And so, in 1898, the federal government forcibly closed—they believed forever—the ongoing legal system of the Cherokee Nation. We are here, today, celebrating the fact that they were wrong, so very wrong. The Jeffersonian view has prevailed, and the Cherokee Nation is officially following "industrious occupations and government of regular laws."

Today, we are witnessing the opening of another chapter in a heroic story. Students of Indian history are familiar with the triumphant tale of how bands of Cherokees forged themselves into a political state, created their own native alphabet, adopted a written constitution, and ultimately provided political, social, and economic leadership not only for the tribe, but in a new state and for the entire nation. What is not as well understood is that the Cherokees were not an anemic people given only to simple domestic pursuits, but were a tribe of fierce warriors and intrepid hunters whose conquest had given them military dominion over the great heartland of the southern mountain ranges.

That the Cherokees were eventually to be known as one of the "Five Civilized Tribes" is testimony to their ingenuity. The Cherokees believed, paradoxically, that in change was the best hope of survival as an Indian people. Historical proof of the significance of this attitude is found in the testimony of Charles Hicks, a Cherokee chief and one of the earliest advocates of this policy. At the beginning of the nineteenth century, Hicks wrote to the missionary Daniel Sabin Buttrick that abandonment of old ways and adoption of new ones represented "the [tribe's] conviction that their very existence as a people depends upon it."[10]

There is a widely held belief that between 1808 and 1809, under the tutelage of Jefferson and other leaders, the Cherokees dramatically broke with their ancient law ways and passed from a state of "savage" lawlessness to a highly sophisticated, efficiently operating "civilized" system of tribal laws and courts. To anyone familiar with law and the development of legal institutions, this is obviously rhetoric of mythical proportions. The Cherokees did not, as is commonly believed, break all threads of cultural continuity. They built upon their own ancient traditions. In 1808 the tribe drafted the first written law, prohibiting the execution of clan revenge, but this act should not be taken as evidence that all native aspects of tribal law were purged. In fact, Cherokee records affirm that traditional tribal values played, and hopefully will continue to play, a vital role in the development of the Cherokee legal system.

The Cherokee legal experience illustrates that it is possible to retain a tribal worldview within the context of evolving Anglo-Saxon institutions. The result of the creation of a Cherokee constitution and court system, however, was not what Jefferson and the "civilizers" had expected. Instead of a weak carbon copy, an anemic shadow people, the Cherokees emerged as worthy adversaries who demanded that their own Cherokee institutions be respected. The tribe had been schooled in the ways of the white man, but retained their own sense of Indian values, which demanded that they too be extended the rights to which they were entitled by the U.S. Constitution and laws.

There is a lesson of law and constitutionalism in the case of the Cherokees who took their struggle, rooted in the stated laws and values of both Indian and white society, to the United States' highest court in *Cherokee Nation v. Georgia*[11] and *Worcester v. Georgia*.[12] "In truth," the Cherokees wrote in their 1835 Memorial to Congress, "our cause is your own." The shared fate of all men under law has rarely been more poignantly evoked. The Cherokees proclaimed: "It is the cause of liberty and justice. It is based upon your own principles, which we have learned from yourself; for we have gloried to count your Washington and your Jefferson our great teachers."[13]

The Cherokee experience demonstrates that law is more—much more—than powdered wigs, black robes, leather-bound statutes, silver stars, and blinded ladies with balanced scales. Law is also a Cherokee religious leader listening to the spirit world while holding the sacred wampums in hand, just as it is the Cheyenne Soldier–Society warrior draped in the skin of a wolf. In fact, a command from the spirit world can have greater force as law than the most elaborate of codes devised by the most learned of men. For law is organic. Law is part of a time and a place, the product of a specific time and an actual place. Thus law was to the traditional Cherokee a part of a larger worldview, a command from the spirit world. And it is as such that we must view the law of the Cherokees.

Despite the pronouncements of long-winded professors like myself or high-priced lawyers—none of whom are here today—law is really in the final analysis about "doing the right thing," about creating a social order rooted in the basic values of people. The Cherokee experience offers a powerful message about cultural persistence and change. As the world moves toward the twenty-first century, this vision of the eighteenth- and nineteenth-century Cherokee can help all mankind appreciate the dual task of preserving historic values while building new traditions. This can help in understanding the universal challenge of responding to cultural and technological change while continuing "to do the right thing."

John Haywood, in his *Natural and Aboriginal History of Tennessee*,[14] describes the Cherokees of the eighteenth century gathered together to hear the recitation of their ancient laws. Historic photographs record the nineteenth-century Cherokee chiefs in the act of delivering their annual messages here in this square at Tahlequah. Today, before this capitol, Cherokees are once again gathered to talk about law. Over the past three centuries the outward manifestation of Cherokee law and the forms of address have changed, but the values central to law—the shared consensus of common ideals, the command to do the right thing—remains the same.

Today is one of those days when you hope that life is like in the movies—like in those movies where at the end of the film all of the characters who fought the noble fight, suffered bitter disappointment, and have been called to a heavenly kingdom are brought back across the screen with their faces superimposed upon the triumphant climax that they did not live to see. When that picture comes to my mind's eye, I think of Mary, the Cherokee woman about whom Edward Everett Dale, the dean of Oklahoma's territorial historians, wrote. This Cherokee woman, married to a non-Indian man, refused to attend the 1907 Oklahoma statehood ceremonies with her husband. He returned to Tahlequah and said to her: "Well, Mary, we no longer live in the Cherokee Nation." Tears came to her eyes thirty years later as she recalled that day. "It broke my heart. I went to bed and cried all night long. It seemed more than I could bear that the Cherokee Nation, my country and my people's country was no more."[15] *Not so!* On this historic day, the Cherokee Nation is making a statement. It is reaffirming the faith of the thousands of historic Marys and Redbirds and Cecils who never ever surrendered their love of Nation. The statement is that the nation is *evermore.* The eternal flame of the Cherokees is more than metaphor, it is truth.

On this historic day, we all hold in our hearts many individuals whom we wish were here with us today to share in our celebration. Without many of those men and women who made personal and historic sacrifices, this symbolic day would not be possible. If you will forgive me a personal note of pride, as a teacher, I am touched to see the contributions of many of my students, Cherokees who have become a part of this rebirth: Phillip Viles, who was a key figure in the preparation of constitutional documents and also an early member and Chief Justice of the revitalized Cherokee Supreme Court; Chad Smith, who drafted much of the new Cherokee Code; Tina Jordan, who is the first judge of this new Cherokee court; Joel Thompson of the Cherokee Housing Authority. And others, the students of many others, who have contributed so much and will continue to contribute even more.

Looking at this platform party, we see Chief Mankiller, who symbolizes the historic role of the "Beloved Women" of Cherokee tradition and the gifted world-traveling chief of contemporary achievement; Ross Swimmer, who, like earlier Cherokees Senator Robert L. Owen, Admiral Jocko Clark, Houston B. Teehee, and Congressman W. W. Hastings, symbolizes the continuing national contribution of Cherokee people; and Judge William Bliss, who represents the recognition in this community that the Cherokees and Cherokee County and the entire state are tied together, that what benefits one benefits all, that the rebirth of Cherokee law, culture, and prosperity has been a rebirth, not just for Indian people, but for the entire region. Jobs talk and because of the Cherokees there is a lot of new conversation in eastern Oklahoma. If you'll pardon a slightly political aside, I wish the Oklahoma Tax Commission could learn the lesson that we knew here, in Tahlequah, even back in the days when I was an undergraduate student at Northeastern State College (which began in the nineteenth century as our Cherokee seminary). This is the lesson that Jefferson offered as far back as 1809. It is the lesson that the Indian's pursuit of law and industry benefits the entire populace. It is the message of Redbird Smith, from the dark days of the federal interdict, that there is a "special mission" and a "designed purpose."

In the light of the present-day global struggles of tribal peoples around the world, it seems somehow appropriate to close with a statement of the exiled Polish poet Czeslaw Milosz in his Nobel lecture:

Those who are alive receive a mandate from those who are silent forever. They can fulfill their duties only by trying to reconstruct precisely [the Spirit of] things.[16]

Toward the close of the third decade of the nineteenth century, when the Cherokee Nation began to publish a newspaper, the name *Phoenix* was selected for the masthead. Today, October 12, 1991, it is clear, once again, why that was an appropriate choice. The power of that ancient mystical bird who was consumed by fire and arose from his own ashes is inborn in the soul of the Cherokee people. The Cherokees are remarkable, having survived in the face of overwhelming odds. The Cherokee accomplishment we celebrate today is eloquent testimony to what William Faulkner described in his Nobel address as the enduring spirit of mankind. The Cherokee story is proof that humanity will not only prevail, but triumph.

Could this be "the designed purpose," the "particular mission," the "Cherokee contribution to mankind" which sustained Redbird Smith and his thousands of followers in those dark days? Today, for all Americans, there is a pragmatic as well as a philosophical reason for seeking to find this Cherokee spirit. For that spirit may help redefine the American image, help America rediscover traditional values in this world of change.

How can the nation learn what the Cherokee has to offer? We can begin by teaching the philosophy, religion, art, literature, music, and dance of the Native American. The tribe is already beginning the task of creating such a curriculum. The story of the Indian is the literature of America. It is not trite to say that the Indian sings the song of our forests, of our birds, of our souls. His world is our world. He is of America. And he is America. Why, indeed, are the tales of the Brothers Grimm, Hans Christian Andersen, and the politically minded Mother Goose a better fare for American children than the friendship of Thunder and the origin of corn?

The British novelist D. H. Lawrence, who came to love America's Native people, said the Indian will again rule America. This has relevance in view of something Thoreau said: The Indian has property in the moon. By walking on the moon, we learned that our salvation must come from the earth. William Brandon, editor of the *American Heritage Book of the Indians*, has prophesied that "The Business of the Indian . . . may turn out to be the illumination of the dark side of the soul, maybe even our soul."[17]

LONE MAN, WALKING BUFFALO, AND NAGPRA

Cross-Cultural Understanding and Safeguarding Human Rights, Sacred Objects, and Cultural Patrimony

For more than five hundred years, Native peoples and their European invaders have struggled over their very different approaches to life and to law. Nowhere is this more apparent than in how people worship. The Indian leader Walking Buffalo (1871–1967) spoke eloquently of these differences:

> You whites assumed we were savages. You didn't understand our prayers. You didn't try to understand. When we sang our praises to the sun or moon or wind, you said we were worshipping idols. Without understanding, you condemned us as lost souls just because our form of worship was different from yours. We saw the Great Spirit's work in almost everything: sun, moon, trees, wind, and mountains. Sometimes we approached him through these things. Was this bad? I think we have a true belief in the supreme being, a stronger faith than that of most whites who have called us pagans. . . . Indians living close to nature's ruler are not living in darkness.[1]

Recent legislation requires that these centuries of difference be overcome. During the House debate on the Native American Grave Protection and Repatriation Act (NAGPRA),[2] Congresswoman Patsy Mink of Hawaii stated quite simply the basis of what has become our national policy: "Preserving Native American and Hawaiian culture is in the interest of all Americans, for these unique cultures are a part of the history and heritage of our Nation."[3] The act is important because it represents the new American consensus about sacred objects and cultural patrimony, a consensus not only of members of the

Congress and of Native peoples, but also of very diverse groups of scientists, museum trustees, and art collectors.[4] That consensus is: The sacred culture of Native American and Native Hawaiians is a living heritage. This culture is a vital part of the ongoing lifeways of the United States, and as such, must be respected, protected, and treated as a living spiritual entity—not as a remnant museum specimen.

I hope to facilitate an understanding of Native American approaches to sacred objects and cultural patrimony while suggesting an appropriate tribal context in which to reach decisions consistent with the intended purpose of NAGPRA. The heart of this analysis is a review of the many ways in which Native Americans perceive the relationship of religion, culture, and art. The thesis is that Native Americans, through their own codes of law and Indian tribal courts, are the best prepared decision makers to evaluate factual issues. Therefore, Indian tribes have an obligation to adopt and enforce their own Native arts, religion, and culture codes. By enacting such legislation most factual and interpretative issues can be resolved at a tribal level, which will then provide a historical and cultural record as the basis for potential action by the Review Committee and the courts.

The enactment of NAGPRA brought to an end almost five hundred years of conflict about culture.[5] The debate about European and Native American lifeways began with such questions as whether or not the original inhabitants of the Americas were a human or a subhuman species. Columbus, after all, was on a mission from Spain's Catholic majesties, and the question of whether the Native people possessed a soul was crucial to true salvation. The debate continued in ecclesiastical and governmental circles and resulted in such absurd federal policies as "renaming" Indians; outlawing "heathenish practices," including medicine men, dances, and traditional burials; as well as such tragic episodes as removal and allotments of tribal lands designed to convert Indians into dirt farmers.[6]

Similarly, the collections of human remains gathered for the cranial studies at the Smithsonian are but one example of a relatively recent variant on the human or subhuman debate.[7] Certainly, the ironic desire to "Americanize the American Indian" reflects this ethnocentric concept of the "civilized" European versus the "savage" Native American.[8] In 1990, newly enacted policies on religious or sacred objects and patrimonial resources signaled a dramatic recognition of the vitality of Native peoples and mandated an effort to understand the Indian's own worldview.

Throughout much of American history, the question for Indian tribes has not been one of cultural understanding and interpretation, but has been one of actual physical survival. Starvation, massacre, plague, and military ambush dominated much of historic tribal life. Assaults on religion and culture were equally relentless, but less immediately threatening. The magnitude of this historic holocaust was summarized by Russell Thornton:

[T]he European expansion throughout North America during the sixteenth, seventeenth, and eighteenth centuries produced a demographic collapse of American Indians, primarily because of disease, warfare and destruction of Indian ways of life. The removal and relocation of Indians also contributed to the collapse. . . . The collapse was so severe by 1800 that the total United States Indian population had been reduced to 600,000 from 5+ million in three centuries. Meanwhile, the non-Indian population of the United States had increased to over 5 million.[9]

The nineteenth century was even more devastating in terms of Native survival. Thornton recognized that "the already decimated American Indian population . . . declined . . . from about 600,000 in 1800 to a mere 250,000 between 1890 and 1900."[10] Yet, during this same time period, the non-Indian population blossomed from a mere 5 million in 1800 to more than 75 million in 1900. Is it any wonder that the Creek chief Pleasant Porter called the Indian a people "on the road to disappearance?"[11]

Although NAGPRA officially draws tribal culturecide to an end, the task of implementing the new policy, particularly with regard to sacred objects and cultural patrimony, will require much cross-cultural understanding. Fortunately, the consensus nature of NAGPRA, and the compromise on the part of all interested parties, suggests a willingness to recognize the cultural differences between Natives and non-Natives and within the Native community itself. This is, indeed, the great challenge of implementing NAGPRA. Native peoples have eloquently made the case that compelled the adoption of the Native American Graves Protection and Repatriation Act. This "hugely important legislation," as described by Senator Daniel Moynihan, was thought of by its advocates as human rights legislation.[12] Indeed, Congressman Morris Udall argued that NAGPRA "addresses our civility, and our common decency."[13] He concluded: "In the larger scope of history, this is a small thing. In the smaller scope of conscience, it may be the biggest thing we have ever done."[14]

The spotlight of conscience and the duty of advocacy has now shifted from Congress, museums and collectors, and the scientific community back to Native peoples and the Indian community. The human rights of Alaska Natives, Indian peoples, and Native Hawaiians are now, under the terms of NAGPRA, back in their own hands. The passage of the legislation, even in the compromised and modified consensus form, brought an end to a long, bitter debate and was a great victory.[15] With victory comes responsibility, and that responsibility is to construct a system of law within the structure of Native tribal governments, courts, and legislative powers that will help all citizens fulfill the mandate of NAGPRA. It would, indeed, be a tragedy if the Native community failed in their task. NAGPRA is not self-actuating, but mandates Native group action if its purposes are to be fulfilled. An important threshold consideration, indeed the basis for NAGPRA itself, is the recognition that Native Americans and Hawaiians—tribes, bands, and villages—are legal, living cultures with vital ongoing lifeways rooted in a rich traditional heritage.

Courts have long recognized that governments of the original American inhabitants remain active governmental entities possessing legal sovereignty. They have been continually recognized by the United States as participants in ongoing government-to-government relationships. For example, federally recognized Indian groups possess the power to enact their own laws and operate their own court systems. Within the scope of these rights, and under their own laws, Indian peoples continue to practice lifeways and cultures whose heritage runs back to ages before Columbus. This is the fundamental legal basis upon which the Native American Graves Protection and Repatriation Act builds.

NAGPRA recognizes that Native peoples are not themselves museum objects of dead cultures or even isolated remnants of quaint lost tribes; they are members of ongoing governmental, social, economic, religious, and political units. Native peoples are free under the law to define themselves and their lifeways, including their own legal system's definition of what is a sacred object, what is cultural patrimony, what property may be transferred by individuals, and what property can be alienated or placed in trust only by the entire tribal group.

The language of NAGPRA is quite clear about the role of Native legal concepts, particularly in the definition of the terms *sacred objects, cultural patrimony,* and *rights of possession.*[16] *Sacred objects* includes specific ceremonial objects that are needed by traditional Native American religious leaders for the purpose of practicing traditional Native American religions by their present-day adherents.[17] *Cultural patrimony* includes objects that have ongoing historical, traditional, or cultural importance central to the Native American group or culture itself. It stands in contrast to property owned by an individual Native American. Cultural patrimony cannot be alienated, appropriated, or conveyed, regardless of whether or not the individual is a member of the Indian tribe or Native Hawaiian organization.[18] Moreover, objects of cultural patrimony must have been considered inalienable by the Native American group at the time the object was separated from such group.[19]

The question of *ownership* or *right of possession* is also cast in terms of Native

American legal culture, a tribe's own concept of property, and authority of alienation.[20] Right of possession is defined in NAGPRA as possession obtained with the voluntary consent of an individual or group that had authority of alienation. The original acquisition of a Native American unassociated funerary object, sacred object, or object of cultural patrimony from an Indian tribe or Native Hawaiian organization, with the voluntary consent of an individual or group with authority to alienate such objects, is deemed to give right of possession of that object, unless the phrase so defined would result in a fifth amendment taking.[21]

Thus, the interpretation and enforcement of NAGPRA as it relates to sacred objects, cultural patrimony, and unassociated funerary objects requires an understanding of the nature of traditional Native American life and lifeways, as well as the operation of traditional law and tribal courts among Native peoples. NAGPRA has placed the primary task of factual determination within the Native culture itself. This is consistent with the underlying principles of American jurisprudence because the Native American is, in fact, the only source of accurate and meaningful interpretation of the traditional aspects of Native culture. Furthermore, existing Indian tribal courts provide an effective mechanism through which these legal determinations can most accurately be adjudicated.

Neill H. Alford, Jr., the distinguished American authority on trusts, describes many of the differences in cultural attitudes as those of "apple societies" and "orange societies."[22] In apple societies: law, religion, art, economics, and all other aspects of society are a part of a single whole, an integrated oneness.[23] In orange societies: law, religion, art, and economics are each a segment; life is fragmented into separate sections or compartments.[24] An apple society does not make the same kinds of rigid distinctions between art and religion that orange societies believe to be absolutes. It is often difficult for these two societies to understand each other because their fundamental approaches to life are opposite ends of the scale of perception. In terms of judicial systems, the Anglo-American common law represents, in Alford's analysis, the classic case of law in an orange culture; Native Americans and their legal systems are apple societies in an almost pure form. And yet, as Alford has noted, there are points at which differing societal paths may lead to the same ultimate destination.

Native Americans see the world holistically, that is, as an organic or unified whole, whose parts are totally interdependent and whose reality is greater than the sum of those parts.[25] Traditional European thought classified all things as living or dead, scaling them progressively from the lowly beast to the virtuous archangel. American Indian thought conceives of all worlds—natural and supernatural, ancestral and contemporary—and their inhabitants as simultaneous, coequal, and balanced. Where Europeans saw contradiction, the

American Indian saw compatibility and, thereby, evaded the shackling of the imagination in Western traps of dialectical opposition.

Understanding the sacredness of the art objects of a holistic people requires a holistic view. Certain underlying principles, such as holistic integration of life within art, are held in common among Native Americans. Tribal groups have a distinctive approach to style, composition, and symbolic content. The organizing principles of Puebloan thought, for example, are sacredness and fertility. Hence the Puebloan aesthetic distinction between secular and sacred arts, and between secular concerns with fertility and ceremonial preoccupation with symbolic fertility. Northwest Coast societies, however, use art as a language of social power, creating images that connote aristocratic prerogatives. The Kwakiutl and Haida, for example, are as concerned with the display of economic power as the Puebloans are with the issue of sacredness.

Objects made by American Indians, whose systems of values and aesthetics are foreign to non-Indians, are nonetheless consistent and sophisticated. These works provide a multifaceted window through which to glimpse and better understand the religion and lifeways of the societies that made them and, in most instances, continue to make them. In doing so, we journey into a world where an object's definition depends on its context, not on an arbitrarily ascribed function. For example, a beaded leather pipe bag might be seen as an element of costume or as an indicator of its owner's wealth, but during religious events it becomes a sacred housing of the pipe.

Immutable definitions are rare in Native America. Where Westerners classify quantitatively, American Indians evaluate qualitatively; where Western thinking tends toward all-or-nothing absolutism, American Indian thought turns on relative status. Western oppositional thinking with its north/south, day/night, good/evil, sacred/secular, contrasts markedly with the accumulative integrative perception of Native Americans. To the Hopi, for example, the fine tuning of sensory reality is explained by *Enevoqa* and *Nananivoqa*, or directions between directions, "going all directions," or colors between colors. This is not the same as the concept of "northeast" or "magenta," but is an infinitely incremental accounting of qualities that tend more or less toward dominant expressions.

As the non-Indian attempts to understand the Indian, it is crucial to remember that to live in pre-Columbian Indian America was to live in a time of magic. It was a time when ordinary men sought visions, and from their visions sprang potent knowledge, sacred objects, prayers, and songs that were the crystallization of power. Seeing the universe through the eyes of a contemporary Native American is to see it as a complex whole of natural forces and spiritual beings—animal, human, and supernatural—woven together in a delicate, intricate, and indivisible web. Man moves back and forth from the mundane world to the world of the spirit. Man is not frozen in a single body and a limited lifetime. Performing the Katcina, or kachina,[26] dances of the Hopi, he becomes a supernatural being; singing the Pima deer song, he is transformed into the deer, his ears gathering the sounds of the forest. As America approaches the twenty-first century, an Indian spirit, far older than Columbian explorers, still lives.

Today, Native American patrimonial, ceremonial, and religious objects are central to tribal power and purpose. Power is an ancient and universal concept. In games, in war, in social and economic struggles, man is obsessed with power in comparative force. Which animal is strongest? Which man is wisest? Will the moon devour the sun? Will the gods destroy the unbeliever? How can one acquire these powers? Power means survival to Native Americans. Perceiving relative degrees of strength is central to the Native Americans' sense of self, of security, and of preparation for defense. Objects of power thus become both sacred and crucial. Indeed, objects of power are the essence of tribal patrimony; without them there may be no people.

One of the dramatic perceptual differences between Native Americans and Western Europeans lies in their differing definitions of power. With the waning of religion's sensitivities in the West, power became predominantly a secular commodity that resides in social, economic, and political privilege. To the American Indian, power is a metaphysical reality that permeates the cosmos. All beings, animate or inanimate, possess power in the form of either patent or latent energy, as well as potential consciousness. Power, whether defined by the Lakota term *!Wakan!*, the Maricopa term *Gwistama-tc*, or the Comanche term *Puha*, is interchangeable with the concept of sacred or spiritual medicine. True power, for the Native American, arises from the individual's relation to the supernatural. The strength of that bond results in social, economic, and political mobility. The Native American religious experience is highly personal and inseparably entwined with the world of secular concerns. Therefore, although sacred objects may appear to be peculiarly personal, they also may be highly religious and influence the fate of the entire group.

Methods for acquiring power, and the visible expression of power, vary from tribe to tribe. Physical manifestation might occur in the form of magic implements, fetishes, medicine bundles, charms, songs, dances, and rituals. Sacred power, or medicine, was obtained through spirit visitations during visions, supernatural gifts, ceremonial transfer, or inheritance. American Indian thought revolves around a reverence for nature, but at the core is a cautious respect for a capricious, animate universe vibrant with obtainable power that is often contained within sacred objects. Traditional Native Americans see themselves as delicate particles balanced against a multitude of forces—gods, spirits, supernaturals, shape-changers, shamans, witches, raven-mockers, and prophets. Historically, cosmologies differed from tribe to tribe, but basic beliefs were constant. Central to all tribes was the perception of an organic cosmos precariously balanced. The significance of supernatural power to American Indian thought is demonstrated by thousands of physical manifestations expressed in art; for example, in the gracefully designed—yet awesomely powerful—chief speaker's staff of the Northwest Coast Nootka and Tlingit tribes. Similarly, the call for power radiates from what non-Indians would define as costume: a superbly crafted raven-frontlet adorned with a six-foot ermine-skin trailer created in the nineteenth century by Bella Coola.

Western classification systems are out of touch with the American Indian worldview. Indeed, even the terms *art, art work, sacred,* and *secular,* as non-Indians use them, embody concepts foreign to Native American societies. Among many Indian peoples, all man-made objects are grouped together and referred to as *that-which-has-been-made.* Distinctions between *aesthetic objects, sacred objects, functional objects, public objects,* and *commercial objects* simply do not exist. In a holistic society there are no such lines.

Many non-Indians have a problem in the cultural translation of Native works. A non-Indian viewer of a Hopi figure, a Tlingit mask, or a Shoshone painted hide translates the object into the familiar framework of his own culture. In doing so he confronts the same distortion as the English-speaking reader of a translated Cherokee love-song. The song, translated into English, has its syntax transposed, verb tenses approximated, and inflections altered. No longer a linguistic reflection of its maker, the song becomes a carnival mirror, distorting the delicate thought patterns of its creator's culture. The non-Indian perception of Native American objects requires a similar translation. The visual arts, and the verbal arts, demand a holistic context. It is simply not possible to judge the meaning of a sacred object from a viewpoint and value structure outside the culture itself.

Native American art moves along a scale that embraces both the decorative object and the icon, and all that lies between. It reaches from the secular arts of basket design, pottery making, and weaving through the semi-sacred and sacred visionary arts, such as warrior shields, to the Zuni war gods and Katcina masks that are the body of the gods. Indian artistic metaphor stretches from casual similarity or likeness between objects to transubstantiation, a phenomenon among Native Americans compatible with the Christian doctrine of transformation of bread and wine to the body and blood of Christ. At one end of the continuum are whimsical Pueblo ceramics shaped like opera singers or circus animals. At the opposite end are the true icons: the great arrow bundle of the

Cheyenne, the taimi of the Kiowa, and the Katcina masks, which are not godlike but truly embody the great force of the spirit; they are lifeforms, to be fed, cared for, respected, and invoked. The power cannot ebb from these objects, for power and object are one. In between the iconic and the secular are vision songs and sacred images, which, though not icons, are sacred objects that can conduct power for the reverent, if all rituals are observed and all conditions met. In this category are emblems, such as the mystic buffalo painted on the warrior's shield, that stand for powers received in a personal vision. For example, the Zuni fetishes are small carved animals that can give to the hunter the power of the animal. Images such as Zuni fetishes and the Plains warrior's shield fall between metaphor as simile and metaphor as transubstantiation. They are part metaphor and part pure sacred power. The raven rattle of the Kwakiutl defines the role of metaphor in American Indian sacred art. The raven rattle, when used in the tribal dance, was not an Audubon-like representation of a bird; it *was* the bird and the bird's power, so much so that in the ceremony it must be carried upside down to keep it from flying away.

The idea of object as metaphor is illuminating when applied to American Indian arts, but the concept is essentially non-Indian. To members of holistic societies, such analysis would seem unnecessary. For them, there is a profound association between all living beings that goes beyond compared characteristics. The idea of metaphor is particularly difficult when applied to the icons of Indian society. These figures are not symbols or embodiments, but authentic spiritual entities.

The sacred integrative relationships among art objects, prayers, and ritual helps to explain the American Indian sacred spiritual consciousness behind them. The complex and sophisticated worldview of Native holistic society is vividly illustrated in the creative life of a nineteenth-century Sioux visionary and warrior called Lone Man.[27] Lone Man tells of his experience concerning the acquisition of sacred charms, ceremonial regalia, and the composition of the accompanying song:

> One day when I was on the warpath I sat down to rest. . . . I fell asleep and while I slept I had a dream. . . . My face was to the west and I heard thunder in that direction. There was a sound of hoofs and I saw nine riders coming toward me in a cloud, each man on a horse of a different color. . . . One of them spoke to me, and said they had appointed me to make the first attack on the enemy. He said the man to be attacked was painted red and was standing in the water and then said that if I could conquer that man I would gain something which would be useful to me all the rest of my life. . . . In my dream I found the enemy.

Before the riders in the cloud went away they gave me a charm (wo' tahe) which I always carried. If I were in great danger and escaped I attributed it to the charm and sang a song in its honor. The song relates to the swallow whose flying precedes a thunderstorm. When I sang the song of my charm I fastened the skin of a swallow on my head. This bird is so closely related to the thunderbird that the thunderbird is honored by its use. The action of the swallow is very agile. The greatest aid to a warrior is a good horse, and what a warrior desires most for his horse is that it may be as swift as the swallow in dodging the enemy or in direct fight. For this reason my song is in honor of the swallow as well as my charm.[28]

Lone Man's account of going from vision to song to sacred object to ritual demonstrates the integration of the American Indian religious perception and objectification of holy powers. From Lone Man's vision came an insight into his relation to the supernatural; from the supernatural came gifts: a prayer, a song, and a protective object. Each element is linked to the other. The initial vision gives rise to the opening prayer of recognition, which in turn gives rise to the commemorative power song, graphically preserved in the form of a medicine charm. The swallow headdress, which Lone Man himself created, is made as a part of the sacred circle of power. Lone Man began to elaborate on his initial vision. Lone Man presents the charms and his vision in the *Heyo 'kaka' ga*: a public performance expressing his own vision and gratitude for the richness of his sacred vision. It is, in turn, presented in the full context of ceremonial regalia and song. Thus, the cycle continues and the ritual objects are joined as one.

In Native American culture, even the most seemingly mundane and utilitarian object may have deeply religious significance. The ordinary object may be sacred in origin and purpose. For example, the concept of *container* may be unexpectedly profound in American Indian traditions. While contemporary Americans think of boxes, envelopes, sandwich bags, suitcases, and other nondescript objects as containers, in American Indian thought the concept often has sacred metaphorical power: man, world, and cosmos are all compatibly significant receptacles. To the Zuni, Hopi, and other Pueblo peoples, sacred medicine jars, like the subterranean ceremonial retreats called kivas, were viewed as effective microcosms of the physical world. Fetish pots and prayer meal bowls were intricately embellished with symbols such as rain clouds, snow marks, lightning, and prey animals, and were occasionally smeared with blood and encrusted with cornmeal and ground turquoise to heighten their vitality. Fetishes of horn, bone, stone, feathers, shell, evergreen boughs, and coral, fashioned in the forms of both game and prey beasts, were either attached to the exterior of a jar or placed atop a mound of cornmeal and ground stone at the center of the vessel. Through a hole in the side of the container, the protective creatures were ceremonially fed. The stability of this miniature realm was thought to induce, by imitation, the same condition in greater reality.

Kivas, with their mythic wall murals, became cosmological vessels wherein past, present, and future osmotically combined, revitalizing the ceremonial cycle that harmonized the world. Though details differ, this belief in architectural structures or religiously symbolic containers as cosmological entities is relatively widespread in Native North America. Even the painted tipi suggests it is a sacred container; its figurative motifs proclaimed both the secular and spiritual achievements of its owner. It alluded to the power bundles associated with a unique psyche housed within a living shrine.

Transformation, in which the Native American changes into another being or experiences an altered state of consciousness, is central to the concept of the mask. This transformation is illustrated by the Kwakiutl songs that initiate the ceremonial season and sanction an individual's right to assume supernatural prerogatives. One Kwakiutl dancer in the Winter Ceremonial wears a vividly painted crest mask with flame-colored cedar-bark strips streaming around the shoulders. The carved eyes, ears, cheeks, and nose are all human, but where one expects a human mouth, there erupts the massive, stout beak of a bird. The mouth seems to speak as the man's lips open, becoming part of the spirit's beak. The dancer's movements mesmerize. He soars and wings the audience back to a mythical time, to an alternative reality when animals spoke and supernaturals befriended man. As the dance continues, the mask wearer and the portrayed creature become one in the eyes of the audience. The transformation is complete. The supernatural power came and put its power into the mask and into the one "who had been made supernatural by . . . supernatural power."[29] The Kwakiutl song described the transubstantiation:

I may bring supernatural power. . . . Now this is done, now you have wiped off your sickness, and you have wiped off your quarrels; now you have wiped off your troubles. . . . Now the supernatural power . . . has come to our friends. Now it has changed all our minds . . . I have come to tell, you, world.[30]

Masks frequently appear during times of ritual passage; those socially recognized transitions in an individual's life. Masked beings dramatize passages such as childbirth, the initiation of an adolescent into adulthood, or the ascendance of a man or woman into religion or political authority. In the final passage of the separation of death, masks once again function, whether in the form of the bunched raw cotton burial masks of the Hopi or as an engraved pre-Columbian shell gorget mask from Virginia. Masked beings also personify cosmic laws, properties, and moral principles. Sacred clowns among Pueblos, Northwest Coast tribes, and certain Eastern Woodland groups were the embodiment of pre-social chaos, just as masked whippers among the Zuni and Hopi were the enforcers of law.

The power of masks is revealed in the fine line separating their use as servants from their fearful potential to usurp man's free will. That the supernatural power emanating from the mask may overpower the wearer is a recurrent threat. Historic accounts frequently mention deathlike trances that occurred to impersonators during mask rituals. Fears were expressed that if improperly treated, the mask could take the wearer's life. As do many Woodland masks, the Katcina masks of Pueblos require constant attention. This includes feeding and grooming, as well as respectful continence during handling lest they choke a wearer during a ceremonial. Other masks are secular objects, created for sale or use in social performances or, as with Northwest Coast items, during a public display of heredity crests and privileges. The most powerful masks, such as the Pueblo Katcina, Navajo Yeis, and medicine-pouched Iroquois false faces, remain sacred objects to present-day Native cultures.

The Native American Graves Protection and Repatriation Act of 1990 has made traditional Native Americans conceptions the controlling national standard; therefore, it is imperative that traditional Indian lifeways and attitudes be understood. The central task under NAGPRA will be the interpretation and meaning of a tribe's own cultural and legal standards. Furthermore, NAGPRA requires that requests for repatriation come from the Native community; thus, NAGPRA's provisions do not become effective without Indian initiative. Indeed, the Indian concept of property and the right to transfer title to property is a crucial ingredient of the law. Academicians, museum directors, art dealers, collectors, and all concerned with Native arts are compelled by NAGPRA to follow its definition of an object's historic Native creators, not the categorization of commercial art consumers or museum educators, no matter how well motivated the non-Indian collector might be.

The Native community acting under NAGPRA has a compelling duty and a tremendous responsibility. The tribe is the only unit with the ability to obtain the historical facts and interpret their cultural meanings relating to the return of sacred objects, cultural patrimony, and unassociated funerary objects. Two crucial questions under NAGPRA are: (1) Is the item one that meets NAGPRA's definition of sacred object, cultural patrimony, or unassociated funerary object;[31] and (2) Could the transfer of possession of the object occur under tribal law at the time of transfer? These are questions that the Review Committee and the courts will be compelled to address if a conflict occurs and litigation ensues. Furthermore, these are questions that the tribe must be prepared to answer before seeking repatriation of sacred objects and cultural patrimony under NAGPRA.

At the present time, tribal councils, legislatures, and courts possess the legal rights to undertake the task, but few are prepared to address these questions. I propose that Native groups adopt a code system to create such a mechanism. The system must draw upon traditional religious leaders and tribal custodians of history. Whatever system is adopted, it must be meticulously fair and recognize that the intended purpose of NAGPRA is to return only those crucial objects of religious and patrimonial significance—not all arts and crafts produced by the tribe.[32] Indian attorney Kathy Supernaw and I have drafted a model tribal code available, without charge, for adaptation to individual needs.

The question of ownership of sacred objects and cultural patrimony has long been an issue of international art law, but under both traditional English and American common law and jurisprudential concepts of Native peoples, sacred and patrimonial objects of a culture are most commonly held in trust.[33] They cannot be items of commerce for sale, purchase, or trade in the manner of secular goods. Thus, under either English common law or Native Indian law, a trust is created on the part of all who come into possession of such objects—on the part of the Native American who might hold such an object for use in a sacred ceremony, or by a museum that displays the object as part of an educational exhibition. Neither can possess a marketable title that authorizes anything more than this basic trust.

It is simply not possible, as a matter of law, for individuals or museums to acquire valid title to a sacred object or an object of tribal cultural patrimony. Furthermore, no individual in Indian society can be authorized to transfer a valid title to these objects. Ownership of such objects rests with the tribal group or religious sect or visionary followers. Clans, moieties, families, beloved women, shamans, priests, and others are entrusted with the objects in their tribal trust capacities, not in their personal capacities as individuals.

While legal theories relating to trust, ownership, and use of sacred objects and cultural patrimony may be the same in Indian and non-Indian law, the classification of the objects themselves may be a point of serious misunderstanding and potential litigation. To a segmented or orange culture, such as the United States, objects may seem to serve only one purpose, but in a culturally unified or apple society objects serve multiple functions. Therefore, a single object may have both a sacred and a secular component.

Walking Buffalo complained that the white man "didn't try to understand our prayers."[34] In 1990, with the enactment of the Native American Graves

Protection and Repatriation Act, the United States made understanding and preserving Native ways the official national policy. Nonetheless, the task of appreciating and, indeed, protecting the traditional religion of others—the sacred objects and cultural patrimony—is not easy. The burden of implementing NAGPRA rests primarily with Native peoples who through their use of sovereign powers in courts and codes can ensure, as Congresswoman Mink argued, that these unique cultures remain forever "a part of the history and heritage of our nation."[35]

CHAPTER SEVEN

AS YOU WILL
Through the Looking Glass of Indian Law and Policy,
or, The Challenge of Painting on an Unfinished Canvas

My father, like most Indian men of his generation, was a great storyteller. When we were children, one of our favorite stories was the tale of the smart-aleck young Indian boy who thought he could outwit the wisest of the tribal elders. The young boy planned to confront the old man and pose to him one question. The boy captured a young bird that had fallen from the nest and took the bird to the elder. He held out his hands and asked, "Is this bird alive or is it dead?" If the elder said "dead", he planned to open his hands and let it fly away; if the elder said "alive", he planned to crush the small bird in his hands. In either case, he would have tricked the wise old man into giving the wrong answer.

The elder looked the boy directly in the eyes and said, "It is as you will—the bird's fate is in your hands." And so, I say to you, it is so with your life—it is as you will. Your fate truly rests in your own hands. That is your challenge. That is the challenge that United National Indian Tribal Youth (UNITY) has asked you as Native Americans to address in this twentieth-anniversary convocation. I have been asked to talk with you about Indian law, Indian lawyers, and the relationship between Indian law and policy. I think this occasion is so important and the topic so significant that I flew back late last night from a meeting in Washington, D.C., so that I could be here to visit with you about the challenges ahead—not only the great challenges, but the many opportunities.

Frequently on my visits to Washington, I go to the National Gallery of Art. On one occasion, quite accidentally I came upon a Henri Rousseau primitive painting of a tropical landscape, in which, amidst abundant, lush foliage, was a tiny American Indian wrestling a giant ape. The plate identifying the work read: "'Tropical Landscape: An American Indian Struggling with an Ape,' Henri Rousseau, 1910." At that moment it occurred to me that this artist had captured an essential theme underlying American Indian law and policy.

In reality, the struggle between the Indian and the ape is a genuinely dispro-portionate one. It is difficult for those of us professionally involved in Indian policy to even comprehend the magnitude of our struggle or the low level of importance that Indian law and policy occupies on our scale of national pri-orities. For example, of the almost half-million items in the published United States Serial Set of Government Documents from approximately 1800 to 1920, no more than 2 percent (possibly less) of the documents address Indian issues. And in the Kennedy Presidential Papers at Waltham, Massachusetts, of the 3,351 linear feet of papers relating to the "White House Years," less than 1 linear foot is devoted to Indian affairs.

It is particularly ironic that despite a generally low level of national atten-tion, a great many people not only claim familiarity with, but readily volunteer answers to questions concerning Indian law and policy. Over the years, while on the road, I have been exposed to the collective wisdom of several hundred taxicab drivers talking about Indian policy, and to this day I have found no more than half a dozen who did not offer an Indian-policy solution. The tragedy is that I'm not sure the cab driver solutions are less sensible than those proposed in recent times by the Congress, the Brookings Institute, the Ameri-can Assembly, and the Fund for the Republic, or in an earlier era by the Friends of the Indian, the Indian Rights League, and the American Board of Foreign Missions.

The "Indian question" is a question most often viewed, in the final analysis, from a non-Indian perspective. I am not saying that this view is villainous simply because it is non-Indian—in truth, almost all Indian policy has been urged by its advocates as a policy for the "benefit" of the Indian. But policy regularly emanates from non-Indian sources, which may not be entirely sensi-tive to or understanding of the complex problems involved.

A recurring historical fact is that Indian policymakers have believed, or acted as if they believed, that Indians themselves could not know what was good Indian policy. The so-called Friends of the Indian of the late nineteenth cen-tury blatantly ignored all Indian predictions that the allotment of Indian lands was not feasible. Defenders explain that the "Friends of the Indian" were "well-meaning," but perhaps misinformed. If they were indeed misinformed, it was not because the Indian was silent. I have personally examined more than a hundred Indian-authored protest documents dating from the end of the Civil War to the turn of the century outlining the consequences of the policies proposed by "Friends of the Indian."[1]

A more modern example of articulate Indian protest may be found in the statements prepared by the Pueblo people against the adoption of the Indian Civil Rights Act, statements which eloquently present the case for traditional Indian legal and social controls. Yet little attention was given to the arguments of Indian people that "Self-Determination" and "Self-Governance" programs, inadequately funded and understaffed, could not be successful when they were transferred to Indian people if still underfunded and understaffed; a school with insufficient textbooks, teaching staff, and classrooms is still a school with insufficient textbooks, teaching staff, and classrooms, no matter who is running it; a hospital without sophisticated diagnostic equipment and treatment facilities remains unprepared after transfer to the tribe without additional equipment, even if it is run by a committed tribal consortium.

One of the most eloquent Indian protests against a proposed policy is a small black-and-white woodcut on the last page of the "Osage Protest," a document prepared in 1879. Drawn by an Osage, it shows a railroad car with the name "No Soul Railroad" across the cab of a train running over an Indian figure lying on the railroad track, with an inscription something like "End of Indian" and "Theft of Million Acres." This protest, too, was ignored. In short, the Indian side of the debate has been discredited or, worse, ignored. Indian friends were there to "protect," not to listen to, the Indian.[2]

This is not simply a historical process. Earlier this week, while I was in Washington, we fought an amendment to the Department of the Interior's budget designed to limit the right of tribes to take historic tribal land back into trust. The amendment passed the house by only six votes; just as a century ago the majority did not want to listen to Indians' advocates, it is still so today.

When I was a college student, one of the topics which we debated was "Resolved: If Russia did not exist the United States would have to invent her." The idea was that inventions are not necessarily limited to things like the cotton gin or the electric light, that people invent or create their own special versions of reality. For more than a decade and a half now, since the Reagan election, our attention has begun to focus upon new realities in national attitudes, upon a so-called western sagebrush revolt, an "Indian backlash," white citizens' councils, and non-Indian resentment of Indian legal and legislative accomplishments.

The current backlash is what I call the case of the "Chatty Kathy Indian Doll." You may recall that the daredevil motorcyclist Evil Knievel took a baseball bat and beat the hell out of his former agent, was sentenced to jail, and was denied parole. As a result of this, the toy company that had made an Evel Knievel doll announced it had lost eight million dollars on all of its Evel Knievel products. The next day a rival toy company, responding to a newspaperman's question about its own celebrity dolls, reported that it never lost money because it was diversified, and that it had a wide range of celebrities. It had Barbie and Ken dolls, Cher dolls, the Bionic Woman, the Farrah Fawcett doll, and the Dolly Parton dolls. The secret of its operation, the toy magnates revealed, was that it had interchangeable bodies for its women dolls. All it did was switch the doll's heads. If the Bionic Woman defected, her head would be banished, but her body could be used for Barbie or Farrah or Cher. It acknowledged, however, that it took a separate body for Dolly. For everyone else the bodies stayed the same . . . only the heads changed.

In a sense, I think that is what has been happening with the white invention of the American Indian. Each new generation has tried to change the Indian head. Each has reinvented the Indian in the image of their own era. Historically, the Indian became a mirror. The Indian image became the reflection of the particular white neurosis of that age. Let us briefly examine the process of invention and the modification of the new models of the Indian doll. We have seen the Indian taken, in the view of white society, from Savage to Savior; from object for conversion to model for imitation and just about everything in between; from the devil incarnate of the Puritan sermon to the new age, non-polluting, horseback riding TV public-service announcement and the Carlos Castenada people of powers; from the "Last of the Mohicans" to the "End of the Trail"; from the good Indian who brought corn to the starving pilgrims to the stoic Marine raising the flag on Iwo Jima. All of these images have at least one thing in common; they are primarily the invention of non-Indians and, as such, represent an attempt to define the Indian from a non-Indian perspective.

Increasingly, Indians have turned to lawyers. And this is crucial to Indian ability to counter the backlash. It was de Tocqueville who observed that in America, sooner or later, every problem becomes a judicial one. In truth, I fear that the society really may *not* have defined the Indian problem as a legal one. In the eighties, the Maine land case began to shift attitudes; more recently Indian gaming, particularly in the East among the smaller tribes, continues that trend. This is a viewpoint reflected in a cartoon that went something like this: There was a group of Maine Indians and a "lawyer-looking" government official was speaking with them. The official is saying, "We have found a precedent that has been used hundreds of times to solve this Indian land problem." And the next strip showed the Indians standing before a firing squad of military troops.

Indian law and lawyers are at a crucial turning point. Over the last decades, Indian law has won many victories and suffered several defeats. It is for those victories that the sagebrush revolutionaries and white citizens councils want Indians to pay. The white Indian doll manufacturers are wrong—Indians aren't about to become empty heads on interchangeable bodies. Successful court cases are both the source and, hopefully, the solution to Indian problems. Indian lawyers cannot, indeed must not, allow anti-legal, anti–civil rights forces to wrap themselves in a cloak of alleged fairness and civil rights when what they seek are clearly civil wrongs. Indian lawyers must take the initiative and define the issues. We cannot allow ourselves to be reinvented as the villain, nor can we allow ourselves to be redefined out of existence. There is one fact of life which must be faced—our Dolly Parton bodies won't fit! And we don't intend to change heads either!

To illustrate my thesis about the continuing dominance of historical stereotypic images in law, I want us to look briefly at several fairly recent decisions of the United States Supreme Court. These Indian law cases include *Duro v. Reina, Brendale v. Confederated Tribes & Bands of the Yakima Nation,* and *Department of Human Resources of Oregon v. Smith.*[3] I believe these decisions are based upon the cant of conquest, a post-Columbian technological bias, as well as a dime-novel, Saturday-matinee image and not upon the overwhelming body of historical data. In these three cases, the Court did not really bother to analyze the submitted historical materials, but dismissed the historical evidence with brief reference in each case to the mythological Indian doll of their dreams.

For example in *Duro*, Bill Quinn, a lawyer-historian, with a Ph.D. from the University of Chicago, prepared detailed documentation establishing the nineteenth-century powers and procedures of Indian courts. The Supreme Court refused to consider these practices because the Indian's laws and procedures were allegedly based on superstition and religion and not really law. The myth of the "lawless savage" prevailed. Like seventeenth- and eighteenth-century explorers, the Court was looking for black robes, powdered wigs, and blinded ladies with scales, and when they found none concluded that the savage was lawless.

In *Brendale*, Justice O'Connor determined that the tribe ought to be able to zone and regulate only that part of the reservation which retains "an Indian character"—where people can, for example, grow medicinal herbs, but not that part of the reservation which is non-Indian in character—where there are stores and modern commerce. My father was one hell of an Indian merchant and so was his father and grandfather. Alexander McGillivray of the Creeks was a millionaire trader in the eighteenth century. Talk about legalizing stereotypic images! Indians can't be merchants?

And finally, in *Smith*, Oregon was allowed to refuse unemployment-insurance payments to Native American drug counselors because of their religious use of peyote. The dissent attacked Justice Scalia for his dismissal of the historical and anthropological data which establishes that the Native American Church is a culturally reinforcing, not destroying, force. To Justice Scalia, the demonic Indian of the sixteenth century, smoking fire as in an explorer's imaginative account, is alive and well. The law in all three cases is decided on images—and outdated ones at that. They are not grounded in historical reality and scholarly research, but rather the remembered romance of the Lone Ranger and Tonto.

Today, when I read the historical interpretations found in these and other recent Supreme Court decisions, I am reminded of the White Queen's remark in Lewis Carroll's *Through the Looking Glass*. "It's a poor sort of memory," she warned, "that only works backwards."

I cannot be a consensus historian and willingly pretend that "the Columbian Exchange" was a consensual experience. I am by training a legal historian, and I object to the concept of discovery and western settlement as a mutual or equitable exchange. In my view, Indians gave—Europeans took. There was no mutuality here. One wonders about the validity of the European jurisprudential "doctrine of discovery" when it was none other than Columbus who was lost and needed to be discovered. Nevertheless, it was this "doctrine of discovery" that Chief Justice John Marshall would so effectively shape, in the nineteenth century, into a perverse landlord–tenant relationship. Vine Deloria, Jr., has suggested this gave the Europeans the rationalization that if they were the discovering landlords, they then had only to serve notice to evict their discovered tenant Indians. And evict they did—seizing the lands they had discovered from a people who did not even know that their lands were lost.

These historic images have little or nothing to do with the reality of Indian life. They are fictional creations of the white imagination and ignore what the Indian is truly like. Each historical age demonstrates how the latest conception of the American Indian was modified by succeeding generations of white creators. We could look at the great ecclesiastical debates on the topic "Are Indians people?" We could look at the literature on the "savage demons," the mass body of books on the so-called Indian captivities, the atrocity literature, the "Our Brothers in Red" pamphlets, the "Lo! The Poor Indian" romantic paintings, and the brown toned photos of Edward Curtis, the Boy Scout and Bluebirds handbooks.

One has only to look at Hollywood for each version of the newly invented Indian—from the demonic devil torturing the "good guy" on the ant hill to the equally inventive use of the Indians as a symbol for American resistance to the Vietnam War. And behind all these models is a basic image of the Indian as the vanishing American, the last of the Mohicans, the end of the trail, the camera fade into the mainstream, the tragic remnant of *A Century of Dishonor*, and the basketmaker holding on to her people's dying craft. The important word is *dying*—the extinction of a strange, exotic, endangered species.

The ideological heart of the current Indian issues is the startling, shocking realization that the Indian has neither faded nor died. I suspect that the white inventor has come to the realization that if the modern Indian is going to die, it is white society that must kill him; Indians have no intention of self-destructing. What could not be done with smallpox-infested blankets, frozen trails of tears, attacks on peaceful villages, allotment of Indian lands, imposition of white governmental forms, and legislative termination of tribal existence will not be done by white citizens councils. As Mark Twain said, "The report of my death has been greatly exaggerated." Recent court cases, such as the *Chickasaw* gasoline tax case, clearly demonstrate that Indian rights are alive and well.

One of the problems today is that Indians are not behaving in the forms that white society has historically defined as the appropriate Indian form. White society can define, even tolerate, a second Wounded Knee, AIM, and Indian violence. Such conduct is definitionally Indian. What cannot be tolerated is what the law is seeking to do. Indian lawyers are behaving in a way that the white inventor of the Indian image did not imagine; therefore, such conduct is intolerable. The Indian legal revolution has revealed the illusory nature of the central shared historical belief that the Indian problem was temporary, that the Indian would disappear, and that with him would go the Indian problem.

In historically reconstructing the origins, purposes, goals, values, and motivations of Indian policy, lawyers too often attempt to find a rational legal basis for policy decisions. To illustrate the difficulty of applying a rational analysis of the history of Indian policy, I often ask my Indian law students to logically deduce the major reason for ending Indian treaty making. This usually stumps them because they develop legal reasons with roots in the goals of Indian policy. They almost never face the political reality that only the Senate need approve treaties, but that congressional statutes, used instead of treaties as the basis for policy, require both House and Senate approval.

A further historical reality is that the nature of the American political process is such that "on-the-job training" at the top level of decision making is short. A new commissioner, or solicitor, or secretary is faced with a significant crisis before adjusting to the demands of the position and is retired with the change of administration, just after learning enough to be truly effective. Meanwhile, a great civil-service bureaucracy moves on, impervious to Reagan, Bush, or Clinton just as it was to Grant, Cleveland, or Harding.

The consequence of this erratic legal rationality has been an absence of a single, unified, established American Indian policy. In the *Through the Looking*

Glass companion to *Alice In Wonderland*, there is a wonderful battle scene between the Red Knight and the White Knight fighting over whose prisoner Alice will be. Lewis Carroll's scene suggests something of the way Indian-policy uncertainty may work in practice:

> "You will observe the Rules of Battle, of course?" the White Knight remarked, putting on his helmet. . . .
> "I always do," said the Red Knight, and they began banging away at each other with such fury that Alice got behind a tree to be out of the way of the blows.
> "I wonder, now, what the Rules of Battle are," she said to herself, as she watched the fight, timidly peeping out from her hiding place.

If there is one eternal verity which emerges from Indian law, history, and policy, it is that, like little Alice, we are never certain of the "Rules of Battle." Our experience always seems to end, as does Alice's adventure, with the White Knight declaring to the Red Knight, "It was a Glorious Victory Wasn't It." Consistently, the rules have changed, often for reasons that have little to do with Indian concerns or needs. Boundaries are shifted when gold is discovered; promises of Indian statehood are abandoned when it becomes clear that the Indian Territory has rich agricultural potential and untapped oil reserves; land is withdrawn when railroads wish to move across the plains.

Marquette historian Father Francis Paul Prucha has drawn from the statements of federal officials many descriptions of changing Indian policy. The two hundred years of accumulated statements are shockingly repetitive, resplendent with confessions of the past errors of previous administrations and the enlightened determination of new administrators to correct those errors by ushering in "a new era" and a "new dawn" for Indian people. This is like Daniel Boorstein's description of "the new reactionaries" as those who admit the failures of past programs, but give assurances that the new versions of old programs will work. One is reminded of Ladybird Johnson traversing the West Virginia paths of Eleanor Roosevelt to commemorate the New Deal poverty programs and to build support for the poverty programs of the Great Society— a task being undertaken once again with the help of a psychic by Hillary Clinton.

The history of these federal programs suggests that Indian policy has too often been enacted upon the assumption that there is, in fact, a single recurring Indian problem or group of problems shared by a unitary people known as Indians, and that the interests of separate tribes in widely diversified geographic areas, with varying traditions and resources, are very much the same. This is not the case. Attempts to legislate or administer generally for so many diverse problems places impossible strains upon the most sensible programs and enlightened discussions. For example, the water and fishing resources needs in the salmon-fishing areas of Washington State are significantly different from those of tribes along the Arkansas River in Oklahoma. And yet our historic policy efforts have too often ignored meaningful distinctions among, and even within, tribes.

If I were to select the prevailing characteristic of past policy it would be, as Alice indicated, that the "Rules of Battle" have never been clearly articulated. Even those "Rules of Battle" that have been implicitly or explicitly articulated have been subject to almost constant change. For example, among programs of this century, we have seen the end of allotment, the establishment of the New Deal's Wheeler-Howard acts, the attempt to settle past wrongs with the Indian Claims Commission, the Truman-Eisenhower termination programs, the urban resettlement of Indians, the end of termination, the emergency of the Indian Civil Rights Act, the Great Society social programs, and the introduction of self-determination and self-governance. In the midst of all these are legal residuals of many other programs from the past two hundred years, not to mention treaties and aboriginal rights.

Present Indian policy resembles a great patchwork quilt—the stitching together of bits of new perceptions and scraps of previous policies into a cloth of striking color but very little design. Illustrative of this historic patchwork process was the public response to *Worcester v. Georgia* and the question of Indian removal between 1820 and 1840. The election of Andrew Jackson in 1828 brought a westerner to the White House, and when that election coincided with the discovery of gold on Cherokee land in Georgia and the adoption of a constitution by the Cherokee tribe, the pressures mounted for passage of an Indian-removal bill. Notwithstanding these pressures, more than one million people, in a nation with a population of about twelve million, wrote Congress and signed petitions protesting the removal bill. Yet Congress and, later, the president ignored that concerned segment of their constituency as well as the subsequent decision of the United States Supreme Court in *Worcester v. Georgia*.[4]

Delivering the opinion of the Court in *Worcester*, Chief Justice Marshall unequivocally upheld the right of the Cherokee Nation to exist as a legal entity immune from the laws of Georgia, under which Worcester, the plaintiff, had been convicted and sentenced to hard labor. In the face of other political pressures, however, that decision was of little comfort to the tens of thousands of Creeks and Winnebagos, Sauk and Fox, Kansas and Osage, Cherokee and Choctaws who were removed from their homeland at gun point, and to the thousands who died on the forced migration.

In reflecting upon the question of what happened to the million signatories of the anti-removal petitions, and to the congressmen and senators who spoke out against the removal act, the answer is clear. The issues of nullification, South Carolina's reaction to the tariff, drew Indian support away from the Cherokee supporters such as the Websters and the Marshalls. It was not that the Indian cause meant less, but that the Union meant more.

And thus the Indian dilemma. What were tribal leaders to do? The Supreme Court upheld their rights, but Worcester languished in jail. Should the Tribes remain and resist removal, knowing that Marshall may have written eloquently in their behalf but Generals Woal and Scott sat menacingly at their borders? The cost of resistance might be—indeed proved to be—the death of thousands of their old people and young children. Or should they compromise and forsake land that was, by the decision of the Supreme Court, tribal land over which state authorities had no legal control? This dilemma has been faced perpetually in the Northeast as well as in the Southeast, on the Plains, in the Woodlands, and in the West. The alternative offered by white policy to the American Indian has too often encompassed just this dilemma.

Despite the tragedy of Jackson's failure to support the court in *Worcester v. Georgia*, a lesson which emerges from this historic patchwork is that Indian programs cannot be based upon congressional whim or public opinion, but must be rooted in historical *legal* obligations—in the courts, in the cases, in the treaties, and in the negotiations. This is the answer to the taxicab school of Indian law, to the suggestion that the mere passage of time ought to change legal rights; the status of ownership of land, or water and fishing rights; or the results of arm's-length negotiations and of established treaty obligations. Public policy, no matter how well intended, is not sufficient protection for the rights of Indians or non-Indians without the threat of the courts. Effective Indian policy must be rooted in the guarantees of law, for we have seen, even today in the Choctaw-Cherokee Riverbed case, an example of how legal rights established by the United States Supreme Court can be subordinated in the name of the public policy of national debt reduction, and how non-Indians are paid by the Corps of Engineers for property rights taken but how the policy denies such payment to Indian tribes. We may have come full circle, back to *Worcester*.[5]

History has shown that Indian policy without law is unpredictable, and that even policy with law is no guarantee against an ape turned loose on the tropical landscape. There can be no sound Indian policy without aggressive and determined Indian law and lawyers. But law alone, without goodwill and a commitment to moral right, produces only legal tyranny. The danger of lawless law is at the heart of Alexander Solzhenitsyn's warnings to the Western world.

When General Charles de Gaulle was preparing to regain power in the late 1950s, he was asked by a newspaper reporter to give his opinion of French policy since World War II. DeGaulle laughed and replied, "Policy? Policy? There has been no policy. It has all been an absurd ballet." The past two hundred years of American Indian policy has really been no policy; it too has been an absurd ballet—a great lateral arabesque best captured in Rousseau's painting of the American Indian struggling with an ape on a tropical landscape.

Earlier, I referred to a visit to the National Gallery of Art in Washington where we viewed Rousseau's struggling Indian; I wish to compare this with a visit to the Thomas Gilcrease Institute in Tulsa, Oklahoma, where a giant canvas hangs dramatically in one of the early rooms. It is a monumental painting by the great American artist Benjamin West. Perhaps the painting is so stark, so shocking, and so significant because it is unfinished. The subject matter is an Indian tribe negotiating with Indian commissioners. White men and red men gather in West's painting, talking under great and spreading oaks. Just as the Rousseau painting illustrates the magnitude of the Indian struggle with the apes, West's canvas proclaims that the tasks of Indian law, like all law, remain forever unfinished, that the issues of the interrelated rights and duties of Indian tribes and of white citizens will remain with us always, as much a part of American law and the legal system as the Constitution or the states or the courts themselves.

Indian law itself is one of the most historical of all areas of law. Like all law and all history, Indian law has become encrusted with a series of myths. One of the greatest of these myths is that law itself is at the heart of Indian policy. Rather, the contrary is true. It may be heresy for a law professor, especially one who professes about Indian law, but it is an historical truth (if there can be such a thing) that this collection of doctrines and decisions we call Indian law is primarily an expression of Indian policy. And that policy is little more than the collected value judgments of society at any given moment: a matter of history. Indian law grows from, and is merged in, the historical experience.

The content of our Indian law depends upon society's definition at any point in time of the so-called Indian problem. The fact that we often talk about the "Indian problem" as if it were a disease, a malignant tumor that can be removed like some operable cancer, tells us much, in a historical sense, about how we frame the policy issue, and about what legal solutions society thinks possible. To the historian, the recognition of the very existence of a problem, the definition of an issue as one that requires a solution, and the sort of definition given for the issue are products of a historic time and a historic place.

Our conception of the problem, moreover, defines what we consider to be its solution. Law, a response to these problems and issues, is thus a social phenomenon; it comes into being in a particular historical milieu.

Let us run quickly though prior ages of Indian policy, looking at the definitions of the "Indian problem" in historical perspective. Experience shows that government policy follows shifts in public perceptions of the "Indian problem." We are all familiar with the early Jeffersonian civilization policy, with the age of trading posts and federal factors when the instruments of civilization such as plows and spinning wheels were distributed by men who were officially called "the agents of civilization." We are also familiar with the era when operation of Indian policy was turned over to the churches, to denominational Christianity. Monies were paid directly to church groups to conduct Indian policy. Who can forget the age of military conquest? When the "Indian problem" is seen as a military problem, Indian administration is entrusted to the War Department. And there were the times when the "solution" was thought of as "education," or as "urban resettlement," or as any of a dozen other programs. The important fact is that when we saw the "Indian problem" as one of saving his soul, we turned to men of God; when we saw it as a problem of securing military victory, we turned to soldiers; and when we saw it as training and educating, we turned to teachers.

To appreciate the social influence on law and policy to its fullest, let us look at Indian law and the manipulation of policy in the late nineteenth century. The goal was to assure that white values lived and Indian civilization died. This was the time of forced reservation assimilation, the allotment of Indian lands, and the founding of the so-called Courts of Indian Offenses, the goal of which was to eliminate "heathenish practices." Law and land were twin cornerstones of this Indian "reform" structure. Education, in turn, was to make the program workable. In the final analysis, the earnest nineteenth-century reformers, who called themselves "the friends of the Indians," were determined to use the law to make Americans out of the American Indian. The Indian was to become another lost race in the American melting pot. The Indian was to own his own farm and to become selfishly interested in competing for material goods. Accomplishing this end required a division of the commonly owned and held tribal lands among the individual members of the tribe. Implicit in this program was the assumption that this was God's plan and man's reward. Tragically, not only did it not work, but it robbed the Indian of much that was working in his own traditional culture. It could not have worked, given the conditions of the age and the values of the Indian. The Indian was being asked to sacrifice many of the best parts of his culture for most of the worst parts of the white culture.

In the past, we turned to traders, missionaries, soldiers, and teachers for solutions to the "Indian problem." Today, we have turned to lawyers. As de Tocqueville said, in America sooner or later every problem becomes a judicial one. Many questions of Indian policies are indeed before courts. In truth, however, I suspect that society has only partially defined the Indian problem as a legal one. Older conceptions of civilizing, assimilation, and even military solutions still have some currency. Moreover, from the historian's viewpoint, we are at a "watershed," or "shifting point," in popular, social definition of the "Indian problem." We are at a time when the basic value aspects of public attitude may change.

I think we are now moving into an age where much of society no longer perceives the Indian problem as legal. Social planners are now attempting to fill the role that the lawyer has played. We may see the Indian question not as a dispute over rights with a legal solution, but as a "social problem" for which we seek a federal, alphabet-soup solution from housing, health, and half-a-hundred other agencies. Quite frankly, it is a time in which the Indian leader has learned how to manipulate, and yet is being manipulated by, the no-name, too-many-programs, easy-solution-with-the-dollar bureaucrats. Thus, the Indian problem is now becoming a bureaucratic one and just as the country seems determined to abandon these federal initiatives in so many areas.

In the process, the administrator and the administered feed upon each other. Many of these programs are needed and successful. My criticism, however, is that congressional and administrative dollars and directives establish the categories, determine the programs, direct the energies, and set the priorities of Indian people. This year it may be houses, last year it was juveniles, next year it may be the elderly. My point is that the energies of Indians are too often drawn off by non-Indian dictates. Social planners direct Indians toward programs that the social planners feel are the solutions to the "Indian problem." This new Indian policy is just another form of dollar colonialism. It is what, in an earlier address, I called "the Wild West Banana Oil Medicine Show" because I suspect that if a federal agency were to announce a special program to subsidize the research and development or growing of banana oil that plane loads of Indian leaders might rush the capitol declaring "banana oil is an historic part of our tribal heritage." Hopefully, new tribal programs of self-governance and budget compacting may begin to shift this tendency.

Again, if we maintain that history does teach, what are the historical lessons for our present policy? The experience of prior phases of Indian policy should tell us a good bit about playing with law and manipulating culture. We learn, empirically, that it is difficult, if not impossible, to graft white institutions forcibly onto the Indian body politic. For law is organic, the product of a specific time and an actual place. The nineteenth-century "friends of the Indians" failed because their laws were not suited to Indian values. The nineteenth-century reformer believed that the Indian was approaching extinction, that native values and culture were destined to pass. A sound contemporary Indian policy must recognize that the Indian way is very much alive and well.

We ought also learn that the persistent conceptual framework of the Indian as a "problem," to be corrected by whatever means seem appropriate to the non-Indian government of the time, is fundamentally flawed. We quickly acknowledge the errors of the nineteenth-century reformers and other past "solutions"; it is to be hoped that we will acknowledge as clearly that present-day "solutions"—when determined by non-Indians—are equally flawed. What is needed is a new perception of the Indian, a perception of the Indian not as a problem to be corrected, but as peoples with rights, duties, and powers.

There is a line in an old letter from Western Cherokee chief John Jolly to Andrew Jackson in which Jolly asks that the president "take us by the hand and lead us while we are in Washington for the President's city is large and we are lost when we are here."[6] As Indian lawyers and prospective Indian lawyers, we are, in fact, extending our professional hand to Indian people. This is our job. This is our challenge. And this is our privilege.

How often I have wished, when working in the maze of federal statutes, cases, regulations, and directives, that someone would take me by the hand and lead me through Washington because I too am often lost there. The only thing I hope is that it isn't an Andrew Jackson extending the hand. You may remember from history that when Jackson took the Cherokee by the hand he led them at gunpoint over the "Trail of Tears," where four thousand suffered an agonizing death. We, as educated Indian professionals, must extend our hand while we continue to be on guard to protect Indian people against the hands of future Andrew Jacksons, who are all too ready to direct the Indian people down the modern trail of tears. And, like Jackson, many profess friendship and even ties of blood. Our job, indeed, our challenge, is to know which hands contain guns and which gifts, and to understand that, upon occasion, gifts may be more dangerous than the guns.

In a sense, the challenges and the questions that face young Indians who are considering becoming lawyers are related to the one that has long troubled all Indian people—the dilemma of living in two worlds, one traditional and one modern. To the lawyer the question is: How can I be both an Indian and an attorney? How can I be true to myself and true to my people? How can I be both prosperous and proud? How can I be loyal to my tribal heritage as an Indian and faithful to my oath as an attorney? This is the challenge—the challenge that young John Rollin Ridge, the first Indian attorney admitted to practice in a state court, faced almost a century and a half ago.

There is a scene in Thomas Fall's novel, *The Ordeal of Running Standing*, which, to me, expresses most poignantly these problems. In the initial meeting between C. Jeremy Roscoe and Joe Running Standing, Roscoe, the tycoon owner of Roscoe Oil, puts a proposition to this young Kiowa who has just graduated from Carlisle.

Roscoe put his arm around Joe Running Standing, led him through the door onto a terrace overlooking New York's Fifth Avenue, pointed to the parade of passing traffic below, and asked how Joe would like to have a motor car of his own. A Reo Runabout, a Winton, or even a new rear-engine Cadillac. If his plans worked out, Joe could have as many automobiles as he wanted.

"It is my plan for you to become a lawyer, Joseph."

"A lawyer, sir?" This time the "sir" slipped out involuntarily.

"Exactly. I intend to train you briefly here to acquaint you with the general structure of our company and then send you out to Muskogee, Indian Territory, to work for us and read law under the guidance of our attorney there. By the time of Statehood, which will be soon, you can be admitted to the bar. There is a great future for you. In politics, in business—or in both."

Joe backed away. He did not like for Roscoe's arm to stay around him so long. "I still don't know anything about you, Mr. Roscoe," he heard himself say, and he liked hearing it, for he was surprised that he had been able to say anything in the least coherent.

Roscoe considered the remark and then laughed jovially, implying that there was no reason anyone should know very much about him. "Know thy self, Joseph," he said, "and fear no man."

"Why have you picked me to become a lawyer for you?"

"That question makes sense. I picked you because I need the help of an Indian. To be worth a great deal to me, he must be intelligent, popular, and acquainted with the white civilization. You fit the bill better than anyone Carlisle has turned out in the past five years. I have been looking for someone that long."

"I can only say, sir, that it is difficult for me to understand how an Indian lawyer could be of such great value to you."

"That's another good question. If you intend it as a question. The answer is that a great deal of wealth lies in the ground in your country.

Petroleum mineral wealth—waiting to be drilled and exploited. I can get it out of the ground, but I must have clear mineral titles to the land. Your people do not trust mine, and with good reason. But a new era is before us. I need your help, and in return for it, I will help you make a lot of money. Have you any further questions . . . ?"

"Basically, one question, Mr. Roscoe. What's in all this for me? Exactly, I mean."

"I hoped you would ask that question bluntly. . . . First I intend to help you become a lawyer." Roscoe's eyes were intent upon him. "Then if all has gone well, I intend to make available to you a partial ownership in the Roscoe Petroleum Company."

"Mr. Roscoe, you must admit that it sounds as though you would like to use me eventually to work for you against my own people."

"Does it also sound as though I would let you make a great deal of money for doing it?"

"Yes, on the surface, at least."

A certain glint in the gray eyes deepened. Roscoe asked in a surprisingly mild voice, "Would you be willing to work against your people if the price were right, Joseph?"

"No," Running Standing answered.

Roscoe grinned; perhaps, Joe thought, he even sighed. "Thank heaven. I hope you mean that, and I believe you do." The hand came around his shoulder and again he was led toward the terrace outside the office. "I want you to work for your people, not against them. Always. Together we are going to make a lot of Indian families rich beyond their wildest dreams. It has been said that money is also the mother of good. For wealth is only a means to an end, and the quality of the end it seeks is determined by the quality of the people seeking it. If we are evil, our work will be evil; if we are not evil, our work will not be."[7]

World of challenges and opportunities are waiting for those Indians who become lawyers. We know that, today, the story need not end as tragically as the fictional life of Running Standing. The opportunities are many and the challenges great. Never before and, perhaps, never again will young Indian lawyers be in such a unique position. There is a magnificent challenge and an unparalleled opportunity.

You are, if you will pardon the expression, a pioneer standing at the opening of a new legal territory. The legal work involving American Indian people has increased tenfold in the last twenty-five years. No doubt it will increase another tenfold in the next decade. It must continue to increase if the injustices suffered by Native people are to be remedied. Not only will the number of cases increase, but the dimension of these cases will become more and more complex. For example, we are just now beginning to appreciate the international implications of Indian legal rights.[8]

Many of you have had personal experience with the problems of the Indian Bureau maze. I wonder how many of you have ever tried to "get something straight" with the Indian bureaucracy. With this I wish you luck! Personally, I have had very limited success. I can appreciate the frustration of the catch-22 double-talk in Indian affairs and the desperate need for lawyers as guides in this maze. I talked with one lawyer who was working on the question of the status of Oklahoma tribal government under the 1906 act, which defines the governmental function of the Five Civilized Tribes. He had been told by a Bureau solicitor that the 1906 act was not "termination," but represented "the end of the tribal governmental functions." The solicitor could not quite explain this Orwellian Newspeak, which distinguished the indistinguishable.

Not only have Indian people been treated with indifference by governmental organizations, but the legal profession has too often behaved rather badly itself. On balance, the record of the relationship of lawyers and Indians has not been an altogether ennobling one. In fact, on many occasions, many members of the bar have been at the head of the pack of those who have abused and defrauded the Indian. Angie Debo's *And Still The Waters Run* chronicles the process.[9] There are, of course, members of the legal profession whose conduct has been above reproach, who have been good friends and loyal supporters of Indian causes. These lawyers, some Indians themselves, should serve as examples to us all. I cite, for example, the remarkable life of the early twentieth-century Cherokee attorney Earl Boyd Pierce or my friend, the late Kiowa-Miami lawyer/nurse Ethel Krepps, who helped make the Indian Child Welfare Act work and brought remarkable cooperative ventures together between tribes, medical care delivery servers, and the state and the federal government.

What are the challenges and obligations of Indians who become lawyers? You must be both an Indian and a lawyer. By this, I do not mean that every Indian must serve only Indian clients or Indian cases, or even that lawyers who are Indians should not choose to serve clients exclusively in a non-Indian world. The rewards are great for the Indian lawyers who direct themselves toward legal problems of Indian people. And those of us already in the legal profession have a special obligation to see that the rewards of Indian lawyers are earthly as well as spiritual. We should not, indeed cannot, ask the Indian to become a "second-class" member of our profession, sacrificing family on the altar of service.

There is, in my opinion, no reason why Indians who are lawyers should be asked to atone personally and professionally for the injustices committed by others upon their mothers and fathers and against their sisters and brothers. No cause is served by an Indian lawyer being forced to starve and deny family support because historically Indians have been the victims of widespread abuse. An Indian lawyer—like any other lawyer—is entitled to a fair and just return for professional services. There is nothing wrong with an Indian, who so desires, driving a Mercedes that has been earned by the wit of the brow—especially when, in the process, the lawyer may have opened doors of opportunity for other Indians to follow. There is as condescending an arrogance in the demand that Indians wear the hairshirt and take the vow of poverty as in the demand that all lawyers must wear a Brooks Brothers suit and that the Indian add a turquoise bolo tie.

Several years ago, I got a letter on heavily engraved stationery from a lawyer at a very blue-chip, Wall Street–type address. The attorney was a member of some sort of American Bar Association awards committee and asked me to recommend the names of Indian attorneys for possible awards. I thought this a worthwhile project until I read the next line, which said they were interested only in honoring Indian lawyers who had helped their people *without financial reward* to themselves. Of course, I know hundreds of Indian lawyers who have helped their people at great personal sacrifice, but my reply was as caustic and as militant as I could make it. This attorney, I believe, was applying a double standard. I noted that I was sure he, as an attorney, had served his clients well and that from all of the indicia of address and stationery that he had prospered at the same time. Why, I asked, was an Indian attorney not entitled to do the same? If an Indian wants to work for nothing, and can afford to do so, that may be fine, but I do not believe that anyone who has worked hard enough to acquire professional competence should be required to accept less than others with the same sort of training simply because that lawyer is an Indian.

Let me preach for a moment. Being a good Indian attuned to nature and ennobled after Rousseau will not necessarily make a good lawyer. You've got to first become a skilled and learned practitioner of law before you can be of any value as anybody's lawyer. Just thinking noble Native thoughts, planning triumphant victories, and recounting Indian tragedies won't make you learned in the law anymore than wearing beads, braids, and a ribbon shirt will make you an Indian. Learning to be a lawyer, whether an Indian or not, is hard work. And no matter how pure your motives and strong your desires, you won't do any good as a lawyer if you flunk out of law school. *Let me repeat.* Law school and the study as well as the practice of law is hard work. I've known more than one law student who flunked out of law school while pursuing admirable Indian causes. Law school is a time of preparation. Do not be impatient and sacrifice your long-run potential contribution to your people on the short-term altar of good causes. Oh, how easy it is to rationalize. To a law student, almost anything is better than study. When I was in law school, we used to pretend that watching Perry Mason was about the same as studying criminal law. It just ain't so. You become a lawyer by *studying* law, not simply by being admitted to and enrolling in a law school.

I might add that being an Indian is also no guarantee of wisdom of legal policy or purity of motive. For example, historical research suggests that some tribal leaders might have built fortunes on the removal contracts that Andrew Jackson forced on the Indians at the time of the Trail of Tears.[10] And Custer did have Indian scouts! Purity of motive and compassion for your fellow Indian people is no guarantee of wisdom of policy. Many Indian policymakers with the most benevolent objectives have produced programs with the most malevolent results.

Again, let me stress that being a lawyer is hard work; being a pioneer lawyer in a burgeoning field like Indian Law is even harder work. One does no service for people—white, black, red, or green—if the service provided is second rate. If you don't know property and contract law, you can't be a lawyer for impoverished Indian people simply because you too have been poor or sympathize with the downtrodden. No matter how you cut it, an Indian client is better off with a first-rate non-Indian attorney than with a second-rate Indian lawyer.

A first-rate Indian lawyer is a different question. A first-rate Indian lawyer brings a special dimension and dedication to Indian law. A first-rate Indian lawyer brings not only legal expertise, but can also bring compassion and understanding of a broader dimension. We are, after all, the products of our collective experiences. Could a non-Indian attorney as fairly and as adequately represent the Indian grandfather described to me in the following story?

> My grandfather was an old man. He could remember the old Cherokees. I walked down the road to see him a lot after school. He would sit on the front porch with his red dog and wait for me.
>
> I know he loved me and I felt like an Indian when I was with him. He told me stories in Cherokee. He knew all about the animals and the birds. He could talk to all of them.
>
> When I was a boy, I thought he was a witch. I think my grandfather was a witch. My grandfather was a witch, I know he was.
>
> I remember one day we were out walking and we came to a clear spot between the trees and he disappeared. He just vanished. I started to cry real loud, you know. Of course, he did not want to frighten me. He came back. Now, I was a little boy and he might have been fooling me but I

don't know where he would have gone. My grandfather would not have fooled me. That was when I first knew he was a witch.

One of the early legends taught to me by my old grandfather was that you never plant a cedar tree, because when the cedar tree grows big enough to cast a shadow over your complete body you will die. You know, today, when I am driving through the country and I see a tall cedar tree, I think somebody had died. The cedar tree is a tree of death to the Cherokees.

My grandfather knew when he was going to die. I was sitting on his porch and he walked out in the yard by an old tree that was there. It was not a cedar tree but it was old and tall and almost dead. A whole flock of blackbirds landed in that tree. And my grandfather looked at me and said, "I am going to die this year."

I was only about nine or ten but I believed him. He told me that the birds meant he would die. The blackbirds brought him death. He died the very next spring.[11]

To a non-Indian, this elder might have been viewed as senile or crazy, a man subject to commitment, a man who believed himself to be a witch. To this Indian grandfather, a non-Indian lawyer might have been an object of fear and certainly a person to be avoided. And yet our grandfathers and grandmothers need help, too. How many Indian people have we seen victimized because they did not understand the law and understand their lawyers. As you think about what lies ahead for you, please remember that Indian people need you. Indian people need Indian lawyers and they also need teachers, social workers, doctors, scientists, and skilled technicians.

Let me ride on one of my favorite horses. There is one area especially in which I think law-trained Indians can be of value. You, as an Indian lawyer, can convince both whites and Indians that the way of the statute book and the municipal court is in no way inherently superior to the way of the wampum belt and the warrior society; in fact, Indian ways may be superior in many respects. As a legal anthropologist and historian, I have spent the better part of a lifetime studying the traditional law-ways of the Native American, and I can testify to a unity of purpose and soundness of implementation never achieved by the Anglo-Norman tribesmen in Britain. It seems to me that the white man has always been foolish when he tried to impose his way of law on the Indian. Chronicles of the eighteenth century abound in examples of this folly. John Stands In Timber, a Cheyenne, related an instance of this folly in the case of the sons of Rising Fire.[12]

However, because we know the effectiveness of the Indian way, we cannot afford to reject legal help simply because the offer comes from non-Indian sources. We must understand and work within the framework of the state and federal Indian maze. Guidance can come from good people of all races. For example, the Indian people never had a better friend or guide than Felix Cohen.[13] Those who are so "uptight" about exclusive Indian legal counsel remind me of that classic television commercial, you remember— *"I'd rather do it myself."* There is more to be done—much more—than we will ever be able to do, more than all the Indian lawyers combined can begin to tackle. We need the support of all people and the goodwill of all our fellow citizens. Indian people cannot do this alone.

I used to think enough Indian lawyers might do it alone.[14] But I was expecting, in fact demanding, too much. In truth, simply graduating additional Indian lawyers, even more first-rate, honest, dedicated Indian lawyers, is not an automatic solution to Indian questions. Education of Native lawyers is a beginning, an important beginning, but not the final answer. Indians constitute less than one-half of 1 percent of the United States population. The Indian, as a member of a very small minority group in a democracy, is dependent upon the rest of the population to act with honesty, integrity, and understanding.

Much of what we call our "Indian problem" is traceable to the failure of many good-intentioned "friends" to appreciate the fact that Indian people have an Indian way of life with a Native system of law that happens to work. For even now the Indian is administered by policy and law enacted by the representatives of the population at large. As citizens in a democracy, we must recognize that sound policy should create an atmosphere, economic and political, in which Indian people are free, according to general concepts of self-determination, to preserve cultural diversity, or to promote tribal acculturation, or to extend dormant cultural potential. With such a public attitude, the Indian lawyer can make a truly significant contribution.

As young Indians considering the study of law, you have an almost limitless opportunity. You also face an awesome challenge. Contrary to widely held beliefs, you will not be the first Indian lawyer or even the first generation of Indian lawyers.[15] However, in some tribes and for some peoples you will be truly the first. Regardless of the number who have gone before, you will all be pioneer Indian lawyers in the sense that we have never had so many Indian lawyers who are as well trained and who are as willing to join hands in facing a common challenge.

There was an Osage legend or prophecy which said that the white man would bring something with him that was of great value, but that he would not know how to use it and that the Indian would take it and add to it and change it and that it would then be good and true and pure.[16] Some say that this was

Christianity and that when the Indian joined peyote with this new Christian religion the prophecy was fulfilled in the creation of the Native American Church. I think the same may be true of the statute and case law that the white man brought. Our challenge is to take that law and add to it and change it so that law can be good and true and pure not only for Indian people, but for all people.

STRANGERS IN A STRANGE LAND
Personal and Historical Reflections

The title "Strangers in a Strange Land" comes from a letter written by John
Rollin Ridge, quoted in the opening essay. The first Native American to practice law in California, Ridge wrote from the gold fields back to his Uncle Stand
Watie in the Indian Territory. "I was a stranger in a strange land," he began. "I
knew no one, and looking at the multitude that thronged the streets, and
passed each other without a friendly sign, or look of recognition even, I began
to think I was in a new world, where all were strangers and none cared to
know."[1]

In concluding these essays, I suggest that the last five hundred years are
captured for the Native American in the phrase "a new world, where all were
strangers," with Native Americans as the "strangers in a strange land [that]
none cared to know." A few years back we confronted these issues as a part of
the "Columbian Quincentenary." I believe, from my historical study, that the
last five hundred years of the so-called Columbian Exchange symbolizes the
triumphs of technology over axiology—the ascendancy of industry over humanity. This, in turn, provided the impetus for a system of justice whereby law
was made the instrument of moral judgments establishing the technological
and industrial achievements of the European discoverers as the standard by
which all value judgments were to be made.

This was an historical *transmutation*, which made the assumption that industrial and technological advancement was the instrument of moral achievement and the ordering of all measure. What we have witnessed over the last five
hundred years is the domination of an ideologically superior worldview (that

of the Native Americans) by a technologically advanced but increasingly spir-
itually bankrupt civilization (the European discoverers).

Carl Sweezy, the Arapaho artist, who was born on the plains in the mid-
nineteenth century, recalled the dehumanizing changes forced upon his people
by the Treaty of Medicine Lodge[2] and the Dawes Act.[3] It took the Indian,
he noted, a long time to understand how these white folks wished the Indian
to live.

> When we first sat down on the Reservation, the Agents and those who
> directed them in Washington expected all the Arapaho men to become
> farmers . . . But the Arapaho had always lived in bands, with their tipis
> side by side, their horses grazing together, and with hunting and feasting
> and worship all carried on by the group. It took years to learn to settle
> down on a farm and work alone and see one's neighbors only once in
> awhile. Neither we nor our dogs nor our ponies understood this way of
> white people. To us it seemed unsociable and lonely, and not the way
> people were meant to live.[4]

Like our world, with the collapse of the cold-war balance of power and
economic upheaval, Columbus's world was in mighty flux. The trade monopo-
lies of the Middle Ages were coming to a close; an international economy was
emerging; the infidels were driven from western Europe; the old feudal empires
were collapsing and being replaced with centralized monarchies. In short, we
were witnessing the death of one age and the birth of another.

As Will and Ariel Durant so clearly described, this was an epoch during
which man replaced the cross with the test tube.[5] This was an age and a series
of events that, I believe, began to draw the legal profession into the dominant
role it now asserts in the life not only of native peoples, but also our republic.[6]
It is what Yale's controversial Fred Rodell meant when he referred to "the
lawyer as modern medicine man." As Alexis de Tocqueville, that keenest of all
European observers of America, noted, an American lawyer "resembles the
hierophants of Egypt, for like them he is the sole interpreter of an occult
science."[7] And, I believe, behind this dominance of law as occult science (and
Christopher Columbus Langdell's later creation of modern legal education as a
science) is the Columbian substitution of technology for ideology—or perhaps
more correctly, the making of technology into ideology.[8] More specifically, this
was the creation of a jurisprudence that rationalized—and continues to rationalize—conduct toward Native peoples based on their backwardness, savage-
ness, and industrial and technological inferiority, as well as their failure to
exploit natural resources. From the very beginning, we have rationalized what

the Lumbee historian Rob Williams has called the "Doctrine of Discovery"—a cant of conquest.[9] It is the task which continues to this day of using law as the judge of the progressiveness—thus establishing the legality of the dominant society's value structure. The history of the last five hundred years is a continuous example of this jurisprudential task of defining the nature of the "discovered," that is, the Native people (read "savage") and their rights as recognized in the culture of the "discoverer," that is, the European (read "civilized"). The syllogism is relatively simple but fairly long. It works out something like this:

1. What they do is Savage;
2. What we do is Civilized;
3. Civilized is Good;
4. Savage is Evil;
5. What is Good is Law;
6. Therefore, what we the Civilized do is the Law

The historical legal task of the last five hundred years has been to reconcile the conquerors' sense of civilization and savagery with the formal doctrines of law. In the fifteenth and sixteenth centuries, the so-called Age of Discovery, the American Indian was defined and interpreted against the backdrop of the Classical Age, the romance with the East and the Near East, and the birth of modern scientific curiosity. Early European reports stressed the "friendliness" of the savages, but also emphasized the "exotic" nature of these New World inhabitants. Typical of the accounts of early explorers and travelers are these excerpts from the mid-to-late sixteenth century:

The people are naked . . . their heads, necks, arms, privy parts, feet of women and men are . . . covered with feathers. The men also have many precious stones in their faces and breasts. . . . They also eat each other even those who are slain, and hang the flesh of them in smoke. They live one hundred and fifty years.[10]

The Indian, initially invented by the European, was indeed a strange, exotic subspecies whose voice, one account noted, was "almost human."[11] There were, however, some particularly shocking aspects about the culture; for example:

[It was] [t]he custom for men and women to go all naked . . . And they marry there no wives . . . And all the land and property also is common, nothing being shut up, or kept under lock, one man being rich as another.[12]

Illustrative woodcuts, published as early as 1509, present a fairly accurate picture of the first model American Indian. Therein, a group of Indians is shown cowering while one of them urinates, and in the background others chop up human limbs. In yet another of these illustrations, a wild naked woman swings a tomahawk to kill a European who is peacefully chatting with other members of her tribe.[13] I thought of that woman with her ax when I saw Jane Fonda and Ted Turner "chopping" away at the World Series.

There is little distinction in these sixteenth-century accounts between the discussion of the "savage Indians" and the exotic birds and flowers of the New World. In truth, the Indian is seen as a different but equally strange variety of new fauna. He is pictured with such "strange beasties" as the iguana, the possum, the armadillo, and the turkey. In this age, considerable time was spent among the ecclesiastics and academics debating the question: Are Indians really people? The Spaniards, as evidence in this controversy, noted one particularly bizarre habit of the Indians, which they described in 1565. The habit was "drinking smoke."

It is not such a long trip from the sixteenth to the twentieth century. The twentieth century did not change the sixteenth century view, but, instead, merely gave light and motion to long-standing images derived from deeply entrenched stereotypes. The Indian in the American image is rooted in centuries of non-Indian portrayals of Native Americans—in the high art of Bodmer, Catlin, and Miller and in the popular arts like Currier and Ives prints, Ned Buntline's dime novels, and Saturday afternoon shoot 'em ups.

At the center is the five-hundred-year-old duality of "Savage Sinner" and "Redskinned Redeemer." Understanding the role of historical definition is crucial, not only from the standpoint of the Native American, but of society at large. As long as the Native American remains the "Chatty Kathy" Indian Princess[14] invented by white society, our Indian policy and law will continue to deal with a myth—with an Indian who never was and never will be. Too often, as Barbara Tuchman reminds us, policy is "formed by . . . long-implanted biases . . . mental baggage that has accumulated . . . since childhood."[15]

The most conservative population estimates say that there were 5 million Native peoples on the American continent in 1492. Others have the figure closer to 20 or 25 million. That number of living, breathing, working, loving human beings had been reduced to only 200,000 Native peoples in America north of Mexico by the year 1890. We cannot move on to the question of the future until we have drawn a "moral bead" on the past. To do otherwise would not change the facts. It was Tecumseh who said that whole nations have vanished "as the snow before the summer sun." And it is so.

When Jimmy Carter was asked how long his family had lived on their farm in Georgia, he replied: "Ever since the Indians went away." The Indians "went away"? The Georgia Indians never "went away." They were driven off their lands on what is known as the "Trail of Tears." As many as four thousand died on that one trek. Indians in Wisconsin did not go away, either. Nor did those in Arizona, California, Kansas, Massachusetts, New York, or Virginia.[16]

Genocide is a twentieth-century word for a tragedy as old as mankind. The term, coined only in our century, describes the decimation of a people, of a nation. One of the nice things about getting older is that you have said a lot of what you think, so I want to return to what I argued in *Genocide-At-Law*, as part of the Langston Hughes Lectures at the University of Kansas.[17] The term *genocide* did not exist in the early nineteenth century, when the French observer Alexis de Tocqueville recorded the atrocities directed at the Native peoples of the Americas. As de Tocqueville concluded, in *Democracy in America*, the styles of extermination varied between the Spanish and the Americans of the United States:

> The Spaniards pursued the Indians with bloodhounds, like wild beasts; they sacked the New World like a city taken by storm, with no discernment or compassion; but destruction must cease at last and frenzy has a limit. . . . The conduct of the Americans of the United States towards the aborigines is characterized, on the other hand, by a singular attachment to the formalities of law. . . .
>
> The Spaniards were unable to exterminate the Indian race by those unparalleled atrocities which brand them with indelible shame, nor did they succeed even in wholly depriving it of its rights; but the Americans of the United States have accomplished this twofold purpose with singular felicity, tranquilly, legally, philanthropically, without shedding blood, and without violating a single great principle of morality in the eyes of the world. It is impossible to destroy men with more respect for the laws of humanity.[18]

As a law school dean, I regret that this holocaust was, too often, a "genocide-at-law." Based upon my thirty-five years of study of the documents of conquest, I share de Tocqueville's view that it would be impossible to destroy men with more respect. As Angie Debo, America's most perceptive historian of Indian policy, explains: "[b]ecause of the magnitude of the plunder and the rapidity of the spoliation . . . [s]uch treatment of an independent people by a great imperial power [should] have aroused international condemnation . . . but the Indians . . . were despoiled . . . under the forms of existing law."[19]

Felix Cohen, the father of modern Indian law, writing at a time when the genocidal tragedies of the Second World War were still fresh in the collective conscience of Western man, warned:

> The Indian plays much the same role in our American society that the Jews played in Germany. Like the miner's canary, the Indian marks the shift from fresh air to poison gas in our political atmosphere; and our treatment of Indians . . . reflects the rise and fall in our democratic faith.[20]

I want to talk about the future—as well as the past—the next five hundred years of the post-Columbian world—the next quincentenary. If, as most of us believe, "the past is prologue" or, as the Supreme Court tells us, "the backdrop"[21] against which Indian law must be considered, then there is one quincentennial fact truly worthy of celebration. Put quite simply: historically— *The Indian Survived!* The Indian survived the first five hundred years of the so-called Columbian Exchange. In fact, from barely 200,000 Native peoples in 1890, numbers have risen to 2 million plus in 1990, and more than half of these are under twenty years of age. As my colleague Tom Hagan wrote: "There is no longer any question that a hundred or two hundred years from now there will be Indian people, living as Indians."[22] *This is worth celebrating!* Indian tribes, Indian tribal governments and Indian people are alive and well.

As to the future—the Indian future: Browning Pipestem, our Osage-Otto Indian law colleague, sees the future as a union of Felix Cohen and Black Elk. He told my Indian Law class that he was not as pessimistic as I, that he knew the Indian future would be bright because Black Elk, in his vision, saw the tree of life which seemed so long to be dead or dying come alive, reborn, filled with singing birds. Pipestem, in a stroke of ironic Indian understatement, suggests that those birds just might be Cohen's canaries—freed from the poisonous gas of our sick society—nesting in the tree of liberty.

But survival is never certain. Make no mistake about it. The remaining Indian resources are still the target of worldwide Columbian exploiters. Today, Indian tribal land constitutes 52 million acres in the contiguous United States and 40 million acres in Alaska. Tribes still own at least 10 percent of the nation's coal, and perhaps 20 percent of the oil and uranium, plus vast copper and iron deposits, commercial timber, and "first call" on considerable water and fishing resources. The exploiters are still out there. This is why I believe that to insure a survivable future, we must acknowledge the tragic past.[23]

Enough of the past. Enough of the present. Let us look to the future. I believe that history suggests that if mankind is to survive on this planet, the next Columbian Exchange—the pattern for the next five hundred years—must be rooted in the pre-Columbian ethic of the Native American. The second quincentenary belongs to the Indian. The continuation of the past, the conqueror's exploitation of the earth—most dramatically demonstrated by the theft of Indian resources, the genocidal holocaust of Native peoples, and the wanton disregard of the natural laws of conservation—can mean only one thing. No one, Indian or non-Indian, will survive. We must go back, back before Columbus, if we are to go forward.

We must ask ourselves about the reverse of 1492—the conquest of the conquerors by the ideals of the invaded, the vanquished. What does the Native American experience have to tell other Americans about the future, about his future and all our futures?

The many ways in which the Indian and non-Indian futures are tied together is suggested in James Welch's novel *The Indian Lawyer*. Yellow Calf, the Indian lawyer, is asked, "What do you believe in?" Sylvester Yellow Calf answers, "Well, certainly Indian issues, water rights, mineral rights on reservations, alcoholism, family issues."

"What else?"

"The environment, wilderness, preservation . . . "

"Okay, what else?"

"Generally, the problems poor people face in gaining a voice . . . "[24]

After an extended discussion of wilderness, preservation, and politics, Yellow Calf's political advisor says to him:

"[The state] is becoming one big reservation and all the people in it are Indians. They make noises about self-determination, but we know who, up to this point, determines what's good for Montana—not the Indians, not the people of Montana, but the special interests, the giants, and their backers. . . .

. . . This country is turning a bad direction, Sylvester. Those people you wanted to appeal to—the Indians, the poor people, the conservationists— they are on the outside, looking in."[25]

The Heard Museum recently mounted an international traveling exhibition of Indian paintings called *Shared Visions*.[26] The title was selected because the curators believed that the survival experience of the Native American had tremendous value to the rest of the world as we move into the twenty-first century. The kinds of changes that swept away many of the material aspects of Indian culture are analogous to those sweeping across the world today. We are, as Alexander Solzhenitsyn asserted, at a cataclysmic phase in the history of civilization. It is every bit as dramatic and sweeping as that ushered in when the Admiral of the Sea set forth on a journey of discovery for Spain's Catholic Majesties. Perhaps, as the great Kee-Too-Wah leader Redbird Smith proclaimed: "There is a great purpose for our Indian people. The Great Spirit has not put us through these trials for no purpose. We can show how to do the right thing."[27]

Patty Harjo, a Creek Indian, asks the question about the future in a provocative prose narrative. She reveals the heart of the historic Indian answer.

[Our] ancestral roots were transplanted to a new land of adjustment, grief, pain and sorrow, to a future unknown . . . a future that seemed only a candle in the darkness, a candle of hope for a new beginning. In this land, . . . all cultures and heritages began moving onward toward the sun.

Now our sun shines bright, our future is growing clear. We hide our grief, pain and fears. We are moving on. We try to grasp the good of our heritage.[28]

That heritage of which Harjo writes is a road behind and a road ahead. The corn road, the buffalo road, the Jesus road, and the peyote road are all different, but the spirit with which one follows the road, not the road itself, is the heritage.[29] Blackbear Bosin, the great Indian artist, came close to capturing the spirit when he said that Indians "respect what has been created and they only want to sing about it . . . not duplicate it as if . . . playing the role of gods."[30]

The agrarian poet John Crowe Ransom, in writing about the European invasion, noted that progress defined as conquest has no end. The result is a substitution of means for ends, a cycle in which one discovery, one new process, one new product, automatically and unquestioningly "progresses" to another. When we fail to exert an ethical judgment among our options, we are abdicating to technology our human decision-making power—our value-ordering function.[31]

Appropriately, R. J. Forbes, the Dutch technologist, closes his classic book *The Conquest of Nature* with an American Indian fable. During an eclipse of the sun the stones begin to grind, the mortars and pestles march against their masters, and all things mobilize. Forbes notes, "There is a tendency to catch sight of that same frightening vision" in our times and "to blame our tools for showing malice because our world has gone wrong in so many ways."[32]

Perhaps from the Indian spirit we can assert our responsibility to demand a rational order in man's relationships. After all, the Indian has the humility to admit that he cannot win an unlimited war on nature. The Columbian concept of progress as salvation, conquest as cure, can no longer go unchallenged. We must have a vision of order.

The pre-Columbian Native American philosophy saw a peculiarly strong unity between man and his world. That view continues to this day. Loren Eiseley has written a beautiful explanation of man's relationship to nature that he calls *The Hidden Teacher*.[33] In that essay, he describes a "long war of life against its inhospitable environment"[34]—a war in which "nature does not simply represent reality" but one in which "nature teaches about reality."[35] Eiseley relates the Plains Indian legend of an early people who were poor and naked and did not know how to live. Old Man, their maker, said, "go to sleep and get power [and] whatever animals appear in your dream, pray and listen."[36] That was how, in the Indian thinking, the first people got through the world—by the power of their dreams and the animal helpers.

We know that even today Native sovereigns continue to have a way of looking at the world different from the way of those who worship at the altar of territorial conquest and material progress. As Ortega, the Spanish philosopher, noted: "Two men may look from different viewpoints at the same landscape. Yet they do not see the same thing. Their different situations make the landscape assume two distinct types of organic structure in their eyes."[37] The last five hundred years have been about those different ways of seeing and thinking. In the next five hundred we must reverse our thinking or we will not survive to see the one thousandth anniversary of Columbus's "discovery." In closing, I want to turn to the idea of the Indians' role in restructuring the next five hundred years. D. H. Lawrence, who came to love America's Native people, said that the Indian will again rule America—or rather, their ghosts will. Lawrence believed that the peace America was seeking could be found only from within America itself. America, Lawrence wrote, "is full of grinning, unappeased aboriginal demons . . . ghosts. . . . Yet one day the demons . . . must be placated, the ghosts must be appeased, the Spirit of Place atoned for."[38]

As to the future: As we move into the next five hundred years, Indians are watching non-Indian America. All Americans, Indians included, face the crisis of urban clutter, pollution, drugs, homelessness, crime, health care, and the environment. Events of the next century will revolutionize the non-Indian society of the "car road" more dramatically than old Indian society was transformed from the "buffalo road." As their fellow citizens contemplate a change of lifestyle, Indians cannot help but feel a touch of irony. The buffalo road and the life the buffalo symbolized to the Plains Indian, the upstream spawning salmon of the Northwest coastal peoples, the free-roaming deer that sustained the world of the Woodland tribes were all victims of the European invaders. Now forces set loose by the conqueror have turned upon the latter, would-be master. Is he so unable to curb his wants that he has created a society that will, in the end, destroy us all? This crisis is, in truth, more than simply an environmental one. Civilization faces a crisis of the spirit, a great conflict in basic human values. I believe our only hope of survival is a reversal of the Columbian Exchange; ideology must triumph—values must prevail over technology.

Survival is a word that describes the spirit of Indian people as diverse as the Oneida, the Lakota, the Kiowa, the Navajo, and the Osage. Since 1492, the Indian has learned the lesson of building and rebuilding a civilization, of adapting, of changing, and yet of remaining true to certain basic values regardless of the nature of that change. At the heart of those values is an understanding and appreciation of the timeless: of family, of tribe, of friends, of place, and of season. It is a lesson that the discoverer's civilization has yet to learn, and perhaps never will. The conqueror is not Indian. The conqueror eschews attachment to place and lives in opposition to, not in harmony with, nature. As a result, the eternal values that allowed the Indian to survive have thus far eluded the conqueror.

As a historian, I believe that if there is to be a post-Columbian future—a future for any of us—it will be an Indian future, a pre-Columbian one. We must once again think and plan not just for this generation, or for the next, but as the Iroquoian people remind us, we must plan for the seventh generation. As Patty Harjo wrote, the Indian holds our "candle of hope."[39] Our great hope of survival is an Indian future for the post-Columbian world: a world in which this time, axiology—the superior worldview—might even hope to compete with, if not triumph over, technology. A new world in which we are not all strangers, passing without care or recognition.

NOTES

CHAPTER 1 YELLOW BIRD'S SONG: THE DILEMMA OF AN INDIAN LAWYER AND POET

1. For a general overview of the career and writings of John Rollin Ridge, see David Farmer and Rennard Strickland (comps.), *A Trumpet of Our Own: Yellow Bird's Essays on the North American Indian* (San Francisco: Book Club of California, 1981); and the excellent biography of James W. Parins, published as *John Rollin Ridge: His Life and Works* (Lincoln: University of Nebraska Press, 1991). See also Angie Debo, "John Rollin Ridge," *Southwest Review* 17 (1931), 59–71; M. A. Ranck, "John Rollin Ridge in California," *Chronicles of Oklahoma* 10 (December 1932), 560–69; Edward Everett Dale, "John Rollin Ridge," *Chronicles of Oklahoma* 4 (December 1926), 312–21; Franklin Walker, *San Francisco's Literary Frontier* (Seattle and London: University of Washington Press, 1969), 45–54.

2. See generally Thurman Wilkins, *Cherokee Tragedy: The Story of the Ridge Family and the Decimation of a People* (New York: Macmillan Co., 1970). See the biographies and portraits of Rollin Ridge's father and grandfather in Thomas L. McKenney and James Hall, *The Indians of North America*, Vol. 1 (Philadelphia: Edward C. Biddle, 1836), 181–96; and Vol. 2 (Philadelphia: Daniel Rice and James G. Clark, 1842), 181–83; see Frederick Webb Hodge, ed., *The Indians of North America* (Edinburgh: John Grant, 1933), 1:386–402; 2:326–32.

3. The best account of the Cornwall Mission School is found in Ralph Henry Gabriel, *Elias Boudinot and His America* (Norman: University of Oklahoma Press, 1941). Boudinot, like his cousin John Ridge, married a New England girl, and this biography reprints much primary material on the "Cornwall Indian Crisis."

4. The standard history on the Cherokees in Georgia is Henry Thompson Malone, *Cherokees of the Old South: A People in Transition* (Athens: University of Georgia Press, 1956). See also Grant Foreman, *Indian Removal: The Emigration of the Five Civilized Tribes* (Norman: University of Oklahoma Press, 1932). For the national context and the experiences of other tribes, see Gloria Jahoda, *The Trail of Tears* (New York: Holt, Rinehart, and Winston, 1976).

5. Rennard J. Strickland and William M. Strickland, "The Court and the Trail of Tears," *Yearbook of the Supreme Court Historical Society* 1979 (Washington: Supreme Court Historical Society, 1978), 20–30. See also Rennard Strickland and William M. Strickland, "A Tale

of Two Marshalls: Reflections on Indian Law and Policy, the Cherokee Cases, and the Cruel Irony of Supreme Court Victories," *Oklahoma Law Review* 47 (Spring 1994), 111–26.

6. See Russell Thornton, "The Demography of the Trail of Tears: A New Estimate of Cherokee Population Loses," in William L. Anderson (ed.), *Cherokee Removal: Before and After* (Athens: University of Georgia Press, 1991), 75–95.

7. For the use of outlawry and the development of this in Cherokee law, see Rennard Strickland, *Fire and the Spirits: Cherokee Law from Clan to Court* (Norman: University of Oklahoma Press, 1975), 170–71. With specific reference to the murders of Ridge and Elias Boudinot, see Morris L. Wardell, *A Political History of the Cherokees* (Norman: University of Oklahoma Press, 1938), 16–19. See also sources cited in n. 2.

8. John Rollin Ridge, *Poems* (San Francisco: Henry Payot and Company, 1868), 7–8.

9. Ella Sterling Cumming, *The Story of the Files: A Review of California Writers and Literature* (San Francisco: World's Fair Commission of California, Columbian Exposition, 1893), 17.

10. *Fort Smith Herald*, June 6, 1849.

11. Ibid., Jan. 31, 1851. For a travelers guide with a map of the "Northern Route," see T. H. Jefferson, *Map of the Emigrant Road: From Independence, Mo., to San Francisco, California*, ed. George R. Stewart (San Francisco: California Historical Society, 1945). For a detailed discussion of other Arkansas natives on their way to California, see Francile B. Oakley, "Arkansas' Golden Army of '49," *Arkansas Historical Quarterly* 6 (Spring 1947), 1–85.

12. *New Orleans True Delta*, Dec. 12, 1850.

13. John Rollin Ridge to Stand Watie, Sept. 23, 1853, in Edward E. Dale and Gaston Litton (eds.), *Cherokee Cavalier: Forty Years of Cherokee History as Told in the Correspondence of the Ridge-Watie-Boudinot Family* (Norman: University of Oklahoma Press, 1939), 76–77.

14. Ridge, *Poems*; John R. Ridge (Yellow Bird), *The Life and Adventures of Joaquin Murieta, the Celebrated California Bandit* (San Francisco: W. B. Cook and Co., 1854). While only two known copies of the first edition survive, the book is available in reprint in the University of Oklahoma Western Frontier Library as Yellow Bird, *The Life and Adventures of Joaquin Murieta: The Celebrated California Bandit*, Introduction by Joseph Henry Jackson (Norman: University of Oklahoma Press, 1955).

15. John Rollin Ridge to Stand Watie, Oct. 9, 1854, in Dale and Litton, *Cherokee Cavalier*, 82.

16. John Rollin Ridge to Stand Watie, Oct. 5, 1855, in ibid., 85–87.

17. *New Orleans True Delta*, Nov. 1, 1851.

18. *Sacramento Bee*, May 14, 1857.

19. John Rollin Ridge to Sarah Ridge, Oct. 5, 1855, in Dale and Litton, *Cherokee Cavalier*, 87.

20. John Rollin Ridge, "Fame," unpublished manuscript, Dec. 25, 1847, Special Collections Division, McFarlin Library, University of Tulsa.

21. Ridge, *Poems*, 50–52.

22. John Rollin Ridge to Stand Watie, Oct. 5, 1855, in Dale and Litton, *Cherokee Cavalier*, 85–87.

23. Ironically, Ridge's cousin Elias Cornelius Boudinot became a lawyer and agent for the

railroads attempting to open the Indian Territory. To put E. C. Boudinot in historical context, see William W. Savage, Jr., *The Cherokee Strip Livestock Association* (Columbia: University of Missouri Press, 1973), 64–65.

24. John Rollin Ridge, "All about the Rain," repr. in Ranck, "John Rollin Ridge in California," 567–68.

25. The Cherokees, like their other Iroquoian cousins, believe strongly in generational survival. Lyons, a great orator, speaks in the same tone and with the same message as William Smith, the religious leader of the Keetowah among the Cherokees. For the full text of the Oren Lyons discussion, see Harvey Arden and Steve Wall, *Wisdom Keepers: Meeting with Native American Spiritual Elders* (Hillsboro, Ore.: Beyond World Publishers, 1990), 64–71.

26. Manuscript and Correspondence Files, Office of the Dean, Oklahoma City University, School of Law.

27. Alexis de Tocqueville, *Democracy in America*, trans. H. Reve, 2 vols. (New York: Alfred A. Knopf, 1976), 1:354–55.

28. Letter, Wilma Mankiller to Rennard Strickland, Oct. 8, 1991. See, generally, Wilma Mankiller and Michael Wallis, *Mankiller: A Chief and Her People* (New York: St. Martin's Press, 1993).

29. The entire text of that address appears here as Chapter Four.

30. Oscar Ameringer, "If You Don't Weaken," in Anne Hodges Morgan and Rennard Strickland (eds.), *Oklahoma Memories* (Norman: University of Oklahoma Press, 1981), 163–74.

31. James N. Gregory, *American Exodus: The Dust Bowl Migration and Okie Culture in California* (New York: Oxford University Press, 1989), xiii, sources cited therein.

32. For D. H. Lawrence's insightful analysis of the demon of the American Indian in James Fenimore Cooper and in American society, see his *Studies in Classic American Literature* (New York: T. Seltzer, 1923), 67–92. For much of Lawrence's work on the American Indian, see also Edward D. McDonald (ed.), *Phoenix: The Posthumous Papers of D. H. Lawrence* (New York: Viking Press, 1964), 87–103, 117–18, 141–50.

33. *New Orleans True Delta*, Dec. 12, 1850.

CHAPTER 2 TONTO'S REVENGE, OR, WHO IS THAT SEMINOLE IN THE SIOUX WARBONNET? THE CINEMATIC INDIAN!

1. In 1994 the author located an advertising lobby card for the silent film showing the actors and people of the Acoma pueblo in the film that inspired the Fonseca coyote poster. Copies of the Fonseca poster are in the permanent collection of the Heard Museum in Phoenix and in the private collection of the author. It is reproduced in Rennard Strickland, "Coyote Goes Hollywood," *Native Peoples* (Spring 1989), 46.

2. The following are sources for those interested in Native Americans in film. See: Gretchen M. Bataille and Charles L. Silets (eds.)., *The Pretend Indians* (Ames: Iowa State University Press, 1980); Kevin Brownlow, *The War, the West and the Wilderness* (New York:

Alfred A. Knopf, 1979); Ralph E. Friar and Natasha A. Friar, *The Only Good Indian: The Hollywood Gospel* (New York: Drama Book Specialists, 1972); Phil Hardy, *The Western: The Complete Film Sourcebook* (New York: William Morrow and Co., 1986); Michael Hilger, *The American Indian in Film* (Metuchen, N.J.: The Scarecrow Press, 1986); Hugh Honour, *The New Golden Land: European Images of America from the Discoveries to the Present Time* (New York: Pantheon Books, 1975); John E. O'Connor, *The Hollywood Indian: Stereotypes of Native Americans in Films* (Trenton, N.J.: New Jersey State Museum, 1976); Paul O. O'Neil, *The End and the Myth* (Alexandria, Va.: Time-Life Books, 1979); Raymond W. Stedman, *The Shadows of the Indian: Stereotypes in American Culture* (Norman: University of Oklahoma Press, 1982); Strickland, "Coyote Goes Hollywood," 46–52; Elizabeth Weatherford and Emelia Seubert, *Native Americans in Film and Video*, 2 vols. (New York: Museum of the American Indian, 1981 and 1988).

For a more extensive bibliography of Native Americans and film, see Allen L. Wall and Randall M. Miller, *Ethics and Racial Images in American Film and Television: Historical Essays and Bibliography* (New York: Garland Publishing Co., 1987), 327–41. See also Philip French, "Indians and Blacks," in his *Westerns: Aspects of a Movie Genre* (New York: Oxford University Press, 1977), 76–99; Ted Sennett, "Savage or Saint," in his *Great Hollywood Westerns* (New York: Harry H. Abrams, AFI Press, 1990), 177–99; Jon Tuska, "Images of Indians," in his *The American West in Film: Critical Approaches to the Western* (Lincoln: University of Nebraska Press, 1988), 237–60. See the entries for "Indian Agent" and "Indians/Native Americans" in Edward Buscombe (ed.), *The BFI Companion to the Western* (New York: Atheneum, 1988).

3. This is not to suggest that film stereotyping is excusable for all other groups, or that it does not have disastrous impacts across ethnic communities and among special groups. The practice is abominable and widespread. For a comparative understanding, see the following: Donald Bogle, *Toms, Coons, Mulattoes, Mamies and Bucks: An Interpretive History of Blacks in American Films* (New York: Viking Press, 1973); Donald Bogle, *Blacks in American Films and Television: An Encyclopedia* (New York: Fireside Books, Simon and Schuster, 1988); Thomas Cripps, *Slow Fade to Black: The Negro in American Film, 1900–1942* (Oxford: Oxford University Press, 1993); Thomas Cripps, *Making Movies Black: The Hollywood Message Movie from World War II to the Civil Rights Era* (New York: Oxford University Press, 1993); Lester D. Friedman (ed.), *Unspeakable Images: Ethnicity and the American Cinema* (Urbana: University of Illinois Press, 1991); Lester D. Friedman, *The Jewish Image in American Film* (Secaucus, N.J.: Citadel Press, 1987); George Hadley-Garcia, *Hispanic Hollywood: The Latins in Motion Pictures* (New York: Carol Publishing-Citadel Books, 1993).

4. There are a number of surviving photos of Valentino as an Indian. One is reproduced in Alexander Walker, *Rudolph Valentino* (New York: Penguin Books, 1976), 55.

5. One can get a sense of casting priority from Roy Pickard, *Who Played Who on the Screen* (New York: Hipporene Books, 1988), particularly in the entries for Crazy Snake, Geronimo, George Armstrong Custer, Cochise, William F. Cody, Davy Crockett, and Sitting Bull.

6. For an overview of John Ford's life and his impact on the Indian/Western film, the reader is encouraged to see Ronald L. Davis, *John Ford: Hollywood's Old Master* (Norman: University of Oklahoma Press, 1995). Those interested in further readings on John Ford

should consult the excellent bibliographic essay in the Davis biography, 365–72. An excellent biography of "the Duke" is Randy Roberts and James S. Olson, *John Wayne: American* (New York: The Free Press, 1995).

7. Jane Fonda and current husband Ted Turner have been active in the production of feature films and documentaries for his television empire. While they have been praised for much of this cinematic effort, they have been subject to almost universal attack for the "Tomahawk Chop" gestures of their Atlanta Braves baseball team. Tom Hayden, *The Love of Possession Is a Disease with Them* (Chicago: Holt, Rinehart and Winston, 1972). For Indian films as a Vietnam War mirror, see Gilbert Adair, *Vietnam on Film: From The Green Berets to Apocalypse Now* (New York: Proteus Books, 1981).

8. This excellent catalogue accompanied a major museum exhibition which was, to the author's knowledge, the first public exhibition exclusively devoted to the exhibition of movie posters and Indian artifacts drawing together the myth and the reality. See O'Connor, *Hollywood Indian*, for photo reproductions of these posters. See also the plates in Rennard Strickland, "The Art of Turning Legend into Fact: Movie Posters of Cowboys, Indians and Western Women," *Persimmon Hill* 24:1 (Spring 1966), 51–63, and the discussion of Indian films in Peter Biskind, *Seeing Is Believing: How Hollywood Taught Us to Stop Worrying and Love the Fifties* (New York: Pantheon Books, 1983), 228–45.

9. The Indian community has been sharply divided about *Pocahontas*, but the box-office returns left no doubt that the public still loves the idealized Indian princess. For a thoughtful review, see Gary Morris, "The Incredible Shrinking and Expanding Ethnic Minority or the Roast in the Cupboard," *Bright Lights* 15 (1995), 42–43. For an interesting real-life contrast, see Arthur L. Wilde, *Apache Boy* (New York: Grosset and Dunlap, 1968), which is a photographic/journalistic interpretation of the story of Nalod Clay an Indian Boy "on location" as *The Stalking Moon* is being filmed.

10. Tonto has not been so well received by Native American creative artists. The Kiowa playwright Hanay Gelogamah uses Tonto with great wit in one of his wonderfully ironic plays; the Seminole, Creek, Navajo photographer Hulleah Tsinhhnajinnie exhibited "Lone Ranger and Tonto" at the Heard Museum; and Richard Danay's sculpture of the Tonto and the Lone Ranger, guns drawn before a Sunday School picture of Jesus playing baseball, is entitled "Cultural Confusion." See Hanay Gelogamah, *New Native Drama: Three Plays* (Norman: University of Oklahoma Press, 1980), 65–68. A historical summary of the Lone Ranger is found in Amy Henderson, *On the Air: Pioneers of American Broadcasting* (Washington, D.C.: Smithsonian Institute Press for the National Portrait Gallery, 1988), 179. See also Lee J. Felbinger, *The Lone Ranger: Pictorial Scrapbook* (Green Lane, Pa.: Countryside Advertising, 1988), and James Van Hise, *Who Was that Masked Man? The Story of the Lone Ranger* (Las Vegas: Pioneer Books, 1990).

11. I have heard this story a number of times. The film historian Ron Davis was the first who alerted me to it and he recorded it for the film-history archives at Southern Methodist University. Those archives of thousands of hours of taped interviews are a little-known and extremely valuable source. I am grateful to Professor Davis and to Dr. David Farmer, Director of the DeGolyer Library at SMU, for their special help during two research trips to Dallas.

12. D'Arcy O'Brien, *The Silver Spooner* (New York: Simon and Schuster, 1981), 40.

13. Michael Hilger's superb filmography is especially valuable in tracing both productive trends and ideological slants. Hilger, *American Indian in Film*, 9.

14. The Friar study is more popular than scholarly in approach, but gathers a tremendous amount of data from which the serious scholar could proceed. Friar, *Only Good Indian*, 281–323. Those interested in reviewing the vast number of Indian-related films in the context of other Western-genre films should consult the following filmographies: Michael R. Pitts, *Western Movies: A TV and Video Guide to 4200 Genre Films* (Jefferson, N.C.: McFarland and Co., 1986); Lee Adams and Buck Rainey, *Shoot-Em-Ups: The Complete Reference Guide to Westerns of the Sound Era* (Metuchen, N.J.: The Scarecrow Press, 1985).

15. Students of the films of Griffith regard *The Battle of Elderbush Gulch* as a precursor of *The Birth of a Nation* and note the early incorporation of cinematographic styles that are more fully realized in later films such as *Birth*. The siege structure of *Elderbush* is cited by critic Scott Simmon as an example of the impact. Scott Simmon, *The Films of D. W. Griffith* (Cambridge: Cambridge University Press, 1993), 9.

16. The author collected popular and romance novels that focus on Indians and the interracial assignations. These cover the entire range of sexual tastes, but are remarkably similar in basic plot elements. *Savage Eden* is not an exceptional romance, but absolutely typical.

Cassie Edwards, *Savage Eden* (New York: Charter Books, 1988). This language is taken from the back cover of the first paperback printing. This printing contains a "dear reader" letter, which reads as follows:

Dear Reader:

It is my sincere hope that you have enjoyed reading *Savage Eden*. This genre is among my favorites, and upcoming books I write will include a passionate sequel to my previously published Indian romance, *Savage Torment*.

I'd be delighted to hear from you all and I will respond to all letters received.

Until my next Indian historical romance, best wishes!

Cassie Edwards

17. John Norman, *Imaginative Sex with 53 Detailed Scenarios for Sexual Fantasies and a Revolutionary New Guide to Male-Female Relations* (New York: Daw Books, 1974), 100–102.

18. This original painting was a part of the Indian collection donated by the author to the Heard Museum in Phoenix, Arizona. Reproduced in Edwin L. Wade (ed.), *The Arts of the North American Indian: Native Traditions in Evolution* (New York: Hudson Hills Press, 1986), 279.

19. For example, the author has in his collection of film posters and advertising materials a cartoon one sheet for "Cherokee Strip." Note the entries in Robert H. Rimmer, *The X-Rated Videotape Guide* (New York: Arlington House Publishers, 1984), and Rimmer, *X-Rated Videotape Guide II: 1,200 New Reviews and Ratings* (Buffalo, N.Y.: Prometheus Books, 1991).

20. Selznick hoped that *Duel* would top his prewar *Gone with the Wind,*" and although

Duel was a great box-office draw, it was never a rival to his earlier masterpiece. For a pictorial review and detailed analysis of the production and promotion of *Duel in the Sun*, see Ronald Haver, *David O. Selznick's Hollywood* (New York: Alfred A. Knopf, 1980), 352–69.

21. There are at least two reported versions of the Selznick–Tiomkin conflict. See Peter Hay, *Movie Anecdotes* (New York: Oxford University Press, 1990), 103; and Paul F. Beller, Jr., and Ronald L. Davis, *Hollywood Anecdotes* (New York: William Morrow and Co., 1987), 207–8.

22. The DeGolyer Library at Southern Methodist University hosted an exhibition in 1990 entitled "Bodmer and Buffalo Bill at the Bijou," which displayed a number of the pressbooks and other materials from their excellent collection on film and the westering experience. Both *Apache Woman* and *Oregon Passage* were featured. See the show catalogue by Rennard Strickland, *Bodmer and Buffalo Bill at the Bijou: Hollywood Images and Indian Realities* (Dallas: DeGoyler Library, 1989).

23. Ford spoke often and often spoke differently about his attitudes toward his various films. His statements about the Westerns in particular are at variance with themselves. See, generally, J. A. Place, *The Western Films of John Ford* (Secaucus, N.J.: The Citadel Press, 1974). Harry Carey, Jr., noted the economy with which these Ford Republic/Argosy productions were undertaken. Interview in Lindsay Anderson, *About John Ford* (New York: McGraw-Hill Book Co., 1983), 212–13.

24. Bill Holm and George Irving Quimby, *Edward S. Curtis in the Land of the War Canoes: A Pioneer Cinematographer in the Pacific Northwest* (Seattle: University of Washington Press, 1980).

25. For a scholarly discussion, see Ann Fienup-Riordan, *Freeze Frame: Alaska Eskimos in the Movies* (Seattle: University of Washington Press, 1995).

26. Charles Musser and Carol Nelson, *High-Class Moving Pictures: Lyman H. Howe and the Forgotten Era of Traveling Exhibitions, 1880–1920* (Princeton: Princeton University Press, 1991). The Denton poster was printed by Otis lithographers and features an Indian woman with child before a tribal village.

27. Much of the discussion that follows, regarding early treatment of Native Americans in silent film, comes from the exhaustive research of Kevin Brownlow, reflected in his prize-winning study *The War, the West and the Wilderness*. The author, like all students of film, owes a great debt to Brownlow. Eileen Bowser notes that Indian films "in the early years . . . constituted a separate genre." See, generally, her analysis in the "Indian Films" section of *The Transformation of Cinema, 1907–1915*, Vol. 2, *History of the American Cinema*, ed. Charles Harpole (New York: Charles Scribner's Sons, 1990), 173–77. See also David Robinson, *From Peep Show to Palace: The Birth of American Film* (New York: Columbia University Press, 1996), and note photo of James Young Deer and Princess Red Wing.

28. Phyllis Cole Braunlick, *Haunted by Home: The Life and Letters of Lynn Riggs* (Norman: University of Oklahoma Press, 1988).

29. For comments of Native writers, see, for example, Joseph Marshall, III, *On Behalf of the Wolf and the First People* (Santa Fe: Red Crane Books, 1995); Ward Churchill, *Indians Are Us? Culture and Genocide in Native America* (Monroe, Maine: Common Courage Press,

1994); and Terry Wilson, "Celluloid Sovereignty: Hollywood's 'History' of Native Americans," in John Denvir (ed.), *Legal Reelism: Movies as Legal Texts* (Urbana: University of Illinois Press, 1996), 199–224.

30. Much of the information in this section comes from the exceptional research and dedication to tracking down obscure films of Elizabeth Weatherford and Emelia Seubert. See their *Native Americans in Film and Video.*

31. See the entry on Victor Massayesva, Jr., in Lori Zippay (ed.), *Artists Video: An International Guide* (New York: Electronics Arts Intermix and Abbeville Press, 1991), 139.

32. For the film-actor experience of a Native American, see Marshall, *On Behalf of the Wolf and the First Peoples,* 111–32. See also James Brady, "In Step with Irene Bedor," *Parade Magazine,* June 30, 1996, 14.

33. See Bunny McBride, *Molly Spotted Elk: A Penobscot in Paris* (Norman: University of Oklahoma Press, 1995), 96–127.

34. Kevin Costner, Michael Blake, and Jim Wilson, *Dances with Wolves: The Illustrated Story of the Epic Film* (New York: Newmarket Press, 1990).

35. Russell Means, *Where White Men Fear to Tread: The Autobiography of Russell Means* (New York: St. Martin's Press, 1995).

36. Cornel Pewewardy, "The 'Pocahontas Paradox': Misconceptions and Assimilation of an American Indian Heroine," unpublished paper presented at the Twenty-fourth Annual Symposium on the American Indian, Northeastern State University, Apr. 10, 1996.

37. Morris, "Incredible Shrinking and Expanding Ethnic Minority," 43.

38. Churchill, *Indians Are Us?,* 130.

39. Morris, "Incredible Shrinking and Expanding Ethnic Minority."

40. See the analysis in Wilson, "Celluloid Sovereignty," 220–22.

41. "TNT Film Chronicles Sioux Legend from Crazy Horse's Point of View," *The Sunday Oklahoman Television News Magazine,* July 7, 1996, 4.

42. Alison Schneider, "Words as Medicine: Professor Writes of Urban Indians from the Heart," *The Chronicle of Higher Education* 42:45 (July 19, 1996), B4–B5.

43. Iron Eyes Cody, *Iron Eyes: My Life as a Hollywood Indian* (New York: Everest House, 1982), 154.

CHAPTER 3 "YOU CAN'T ROLLERSKATE IN A BUFFALO
HERD EVEN IF YOU HAVE ALL THE MEDICINE":
AMERICAN INDIAN LAW AND POLICY

1. A color reproduction of the painting appears in Edwin L. Wade and Rennard Strickland, *Magic Images: Contemporary Native American Art* (Norman: University of Oklahoma Press, 1981), 22. The painting is discussed on 78–79. The black-and-white reproduction on 79 is, according to Longfish, right side up while the color plate is upside down. Apparently, the editors couldn't place the painting even if they had all the negatives. Also in Edwin L. Wade (ed.), *The Arts of the North American Indian: Native Traditions in Evolution* (New York: Hudson Hills Press, 1986), 297.

2. José Ortega y Gassett, *The Modern Theme* (New York: Harper and Row Torchbooks, 1961), 89.

3. Charles Wilkinson, *Time and the Law: Native American Societies in a Constitutional Democracy* (New Haven: Yale University Press, 1987). *Williams v. Lee*, 358 U.S. 217 (1959).

4. Vine Deloria, Jr., has combined the skills and crafts of writer/lawyer in such a way that he towers over the entire field. It is the sense of relatedness with the Indian community that makes his observations so significant.

5. N. Scott Momaday, "The Delight Song of Tsoai-talee," *The Gourd Dancer* (New York: Harper and Row, 1976), 27.

6. *Oliphant v. Suquamish Tribe*, 435 U.S. 191 (1978); *Lyng v. Northwest Indian Cemeteries Protective Assn.*, 485 U.S. 439 (1988).

7. Full citations of the statistical materials that follow are found in Rennard Strickland, "Indian Law and the Miner's Canary: The Signs of Poison Gas," *Cleveland State Law Review* 39 (1991), 486–89.

8. Charles F. Wilkinson, *The Eagle Bird: Mapping a New West* (New York: Pantheon Books, 1992), 22–42.

9. The task is underway at the University of New Mexico, with Professors Nell Newton and Robert Clinton serving as editors-in-chief.

10. Reproduced in Wade, *Arts of the North American Indian*, 264.

CHAPTER 4   BEYOND THE ETHNIC UMBRELLA AND THE BLUE DEER: SOME THOUGHTS FOR COLLECTORS OF NATIVE PAINTING AND SCULPTURE

1. "About an American School of Art," *Scribner's Monthly* 10 (July 1875), 380–81. See also H. Wayne Morgan, *New Muses: Art in American Culture, 1865–1920* (Norman: University of Oklahoma Press, 1978), 56–76.

2. These particular umbrellas are reproduced as follows: Scholder, in *Scholder/Indians* (Flagstaff, Ariz.: Northland Press, 1972), 82; Trujillo, in *North American Indian Art* (Pensacola, Fla.: Pensacola Museum of Art, 1978), 42; Buffalo Meat, in Rennard Strickland, *The Indians in Oklahoma* (Norman: University of Oklahoma Press, 1980), 28, and in Jamake Highwater, *Song from the Earth* (Boston: New York Graphic Society, 1975); and Cannon, in *T. C. Cannon* (New York: Aberbach Fine Arts, 1980).

3. For the study of film and restoration, see Bill Holm and George Irving Quimby, *Edward S. Curtis in the Land of the War Canoes: A Pioneering Cinematographer in the Pacific Northwest* (Seattle: University of Washington Press, 1980).

4. Paintings reproduced in Edwin L. Wade and Rennard Strickland, *Magic Images: Contemporary Native American Art* (Norman: University of Oklahoma Press, 1981), 63, 90. See, generally, Joan Frederick, *T. C. Cannon: He Stood in the Sun* (Flagstaff: Northland Publishing, 1995), plate on p. 142.

5. Karen Peterson, *Plains Indian Art from Fort Marion* (Norman: University of Oklahoma Press, 1971), 90–91, color plate 9.

6. Frederick, *T. C. Cannon,* plate on p. 131.

7. Letter, Oscar Howe to Jeanne Snodgrass [King], Apr. 18, 1958, Archives, King Collection, Heard Museum, Phoenix, Ariz., cited in Frederick Dockstadter (ed.), *Oscar Howe: A Retrospective Exhibition* (Tulsa: Thomas Gilcrease Association, 1982), 19.

8. Cited in Jeanne Snodgrass (comp.), *American Indian Painters* (New York: Museum of the American Indian, Heye Foundation, 1968), 11.

9. Paintings are reproduced in Rennard Strickland, "Where Have All the Blue Deer Gone: Depth and Diversity in Post War Indian Painting," *American Indian Art Magazine* 10:2 (1985).

CHAPTER 5 TO DO THE RIGHT THING: REAFFIRMING INDIAN TRADITIONS OF JUSTICE UNDER LAW

1. 30 U.S. (Pet.) 1 (1831).

2. 31 U.S. (Pet.) 515 (1832).

3. Letter from Gane:nu:li:sgi Ne:wadv to Utsale:dv (Chief Thompson), Mar. 9, 1877, Thompson Papers, Cherokee Tribal Records, Oklahoma Historical Society. This letter was published in Jack Frederick Kilpatrick and Anna Gritts Kilpatrick (eds. and trans.), *The Shadow of Sequoyah—Social Documents of the Cherokees, 1862–1964* (Norman: University of Oklahoma Press, 1965), 26–28.

4. Rennard Strickland, *Fire and the Spirits: Cherokee Law from Clan to Court* (Norman: University of Oklahoma Press, 1975).

5. 31 U.S. (Pet.) 515 (1832).

6. Joseph G. Burke, "The Cherokee Cases: A Study in Law, Politics, and Morality," *Stanford Law Review* 21 (1969), 500; see also Anton-Hermann Chroust, "Did President Jackson Actually Threaten the Supreme Court of the United States with Nonenforcement of Its Injunction against the State of Georgia?," *American Journal of Legal History* 4 (1960), 76–78.

7. Emmet Starr, *History of the Cherokee Indians,* ed. Jack Gregory and Rennard Strickland (Fayetteville, Ark.: Indian Heritage Association, 1967).

8. Ibid.

9. Strickland, *Fire and the Spirits,* 237–38.

10. See ibid., 7 (quoting Charles Hicks, in Typescripts of Cherokee Papers, Indian Heritage Association, Muskogee, Okla.).

11. 30 U.S. (Pet.) 1 (1831).

12. 31 U.S. (Pet.) 515 (1832).

13. William Brandon, *The American Heritage Book of Indians* (New York: Dell, 1961).

14. John Haywood, *The Natural and Aboriginal History of Tennessee,* 2 volumes (Nashville: George Wilson, 1823).

15. Edward Everett Dale, "Two Mississippi Valley Frontiers," *Chronicles of Oklahoma* 26 (1948–49), 367, 382.

16. Quoted in Rennard Strickland, *Indian Dilemma,* forthcoming from the University of Oklahoma Press.

17. William Brandon, "American Indians: The Real Revolution," *The Progressive* (February 1970), 30.

CHAPTER 6 LONE MAN, WALKING BUFFALO, AND
NAGPRA: CROSS-CULTURAL UNDERSTANDING AND
SAFEGUARDING HUMAN RIGHTS, SACRED OBJECTS,
AND CULTURAL PATRIMONY

1. Chief Walking Buffalo is quoted in Grant MacEwan, *Tatanga Mani: Walking Buffalo of the Stonies* (Edmonton, Alberta: M.G. Hurtig, 1969), 181–82.

2. 25 U.S.C.A. §§ 3001–3013 (West Supp. 1991).

3. 136 Cong. Rec. H10991 (daily ed. Oct. 22, 1990) (statement of Rep. Mink).

4. Among the groups involved in shaping this consensus or compromise bill were the Congress of American Indians, Antique Tribal Art Dealers Association, the American Association of Museums, the Society of American Archaeology, the Native American Rights Fund, the Friends Committee, and the Association of American Indian Affairs.

5. See, generally, Robert F. Berkhofer, Jr., *The White Man's Indian: Images of the American Indian from Columbus to the Present* (New York: Random House, 1978); Angie Debo, *A History of the Indians of the United States* (Norman: University of Oklahoma Press, 1970); Leslie Fiedler, *The Return of the Vanishing American* (New York: Stein and Day, 1968); Hugh Honour, *The New Golden Land: European Images of America from the Discoveries to the Present Time* (New York: Pantheon Books, 1975); Roy Harvey Pearce, *Savagism and Civilization: A Study of the Indian and the American Mind* (Baltimore: Johns Hopkins Press, 1965); Richard Slotkin, *Regeneration through Violence: The Mythology of the American Frontier, 1600–1860* (Middletown, Conn.: Wesleyan University Press, 1973); Henry Nash Smith, *Virgin Land: The American West as Symbol and Myth* (Cambridge, Mass.: Harvard University Press, 1970); Raymond Stedman, *The Shadows of the Indian: Stereotypes in American Culture* (Norman: University of Oklahoma Press, 1982).

6. For a discussion of renaming Indian and related federal policies, see Rennard Strickland, *The Indians in Oklahoma* (Norman: University of Oklahoma Press, 1980), 36–54; and for a review of restrictions on Indian cultural practices, see "Rules for Indian Courts," in Francis P. Prucha (ed.), *Documents of United States Indian Policy*, 2d ed. (Lincoln: University of Nebraska Press, 1975), 186–89.

7. 136 Cong. Rec. S17174 (daily ed. Oct. 26, 1990) (statement of Sen. Inouye).

8. One is reminded of the ironic tone of Will Rogers's observation that "Indians were so cruel they were all killed by civilized white men . . . " Quoted in Strickland, *Indians in Oklahoma*, 53.

9. Russell Thornton, *American Indian Holocaust and Survival: A Population History since 1492* (Norman: University of Oklahoma Press, 1987), 90, 133; see also Rennard Strickland, "Genocide-at-Law: An Historic and Contemporary View of the Native American Experience," *Kansas Law Review* 34 (1986), 713–55.

10. Thornton, *American Indian Holocaust*, 133.

11. See, generally, Angie Debo, *The Road to Disappearance: A History of the Creek Indians*

(Norman: University of Oklahoma Press, 1967). The Pleasant Porter quotation provided the title for Debo's definitive history of the Creeks.

12. 136 Cong. Rec. S17175 (daily ed. Oct. 26, 1990) (statement of Sen. Moynihan).

13. Ibid. at E3484 (daily ed. Oct. 27, 1990) (statement of Rep. Udall). The human rights dimension of the issue was a central focus in the Report of the Panel for a National Dialogue on Museum/Native American Relations (Feb. 28, 1990).

14. For an overview of the long established debate, and the scholarly as well as popular literature, see Rayna Green (comp.), *American Indian Sacred Objects, Skeletal Remains, Repatriation and Reburial: A Resource List* (Washington, D.C.: American Indian Program, National Museum of American History, Smithsonian Institution, 1989). For the treatment of these same issues in the broader context of international law, see Frank G. Houdek (comp.), *Protection of Cultural Property and Archaeological Resources: A Comprehensive Bibliography of Law-Related Materials* (1988). For studies of the issue prior to NAGPRA's passage, see Bowen Blair, "American Indians v. American Museums: A Matter of Religious Freedom," *American Indian Journal* 5 (1979), 13; Walter R. Echo-Hawk, "Museum Rights vs. Indian Rights: Guidelines for Assessing Competing Legal Interests in Native Cultural Resources," *New York University Review of Law and Social Change* 14 (1986), 437; C. Dean Higginbotham, "Native Americans Versus Archaeologists: The Legal Issues," *American Indian Law Review* 10 (1982), 91; Dean B. Suagee, "American Indian Religious Freedom and Cultural Resources Management: Protecting Mother Earth's Caretakers," *American Indian Law Review* 10 (1982), 1; Paul E. Wilson and Elaine Oser Lingg, "What Is America's Heritage? Historic Preservation and American Indian Culture," *Kansas Law Review* 22 (1974), 413; and Bowen Blair, "Indian Rights: Native Americans Versus American Museums—A Battle for Artifacts," *American Indian Law Review* 7 (1979), 125n.

15. For general development of the basis of American Indian law and the powers of tribal governments and courts, see William Canby, Jr., *American Indian Law in a Nutshell*, 2d ed. (St. Paul, Minnesota: West Pub. Co., 1988); Robert Clinton et al., *American Indian Law: Cases and Materials*, 3d ed. (Charlottesville, Virginia: Michie Co., 1991); Vine Deloria, Jr., and Clifford M. Lytle, *American Indians, American Justice* (Austin: University of Texas Press, 1983); Rennard Strickland et al. (eds.), *Felix S. Cohen's Handbook of Federal Indian Law* (Charlottesville, Virginia: Michie: Bobbs-Merrill, 1982); David Getches and Charles Wilkinson, *Cases and Materials on Federal Indian Law*, 2d ed. (St. Paul, Minnesota: West Pub. Co., 1986); Francis P. Prucha, *The Great Father: The United States Government and the American Indians* (Lincoln: University of Nebraska Press, 1984); Charles Wilkinson, *American Indians, Time, and the Law: Native Societies in a Modern Constitutional Democracy* (New Haven, Connecticut: Yale University Press, 1987); and Robert A. Williams, Jr., *The American Indian in Western Legal Thought: The Discourses of Conquest* (New York: Oxford University Press, 1990).

16. 25 U.S.C.A. § 3001(3)(C), (D), (13).

17. *Id.* § 3001(3)(C).

18. *Id.* § 3001(3)(D).

19. *Id.*

20. *Id.* § 3001(13).

21. *Id.*

22. For a discussion of Alford's orange and apple societies as applied to traditional Native American tribal legal systems, see Rennard Strickland, "Bold Warriors and Turtle Kings: Native American Law before the Blue Coats," in Strickland, *Savage Sinners and Redskinned Redeemers* (forthcoming).

23. See ibid.

24. See ibid.

25. See, for example, Rennard Strickland, "Beyond the Ethnic Umbrella," in Edwin L. Wade and Rennard Strickland, *Magic Images: Contemporary Native American Art* (Norman: University of Oklahoma Press, 1981), which provides a comprehensive Indian art bibliographic essay; Edwin L. Wade (ed.), *The Arts of the North American Indian: Native Traditions in Evolution* (New York: Hudson Hills Press, 1986), which analyzes the relationship between Indian life and art, as well as analyzing crucial issues in a historical perspective. Readers are reminded that this analysis does not purport to represent the viewpoint of the Native American traditional religious leaders, but is intended to illustrate the interrelationship between art and religion and the vast diversity among and within Native groups.

26. *Katcina* is the appropriate spelling in certain Pueblo cultures for the elemental forces who are represented in ceremonies by masked dancers.

27. See Frances Densmore, *Teton Sioux Music*, Bureau of American Ethnology Bulletin 61 (Washington, D.C.: Government Printing Office, 1918), 159–61.

28. Ibid.

29. Franz Boas, *Kwakiutl Ethnography*, ed. Helen Codere (Chicago: University of Chicago Press, 1966), 249.

30. Ibid., 243–46.

31. *See* 25 U.S.C.A. §§ 3001–3013.

32. As Congressman Ben Campbell noted: "This legislation does not include every basket, every pot and every blanket ever made by Indian hands. It refers to human remains, funerary objects, and only the most sacred of religious items which were taken from a tribe without permission. It affords current day Indians the opportunity to determine the proper way that their ancestors be treated." 136 Cong. Rec. H10988 (daily ed. Oct. 22, 1990) (statement of Rep. Campbell).

33. The question of repose, reversion, repatriation, and recovery of stolen works has long been a crucial issue in art law and in the preservation and understanding of cultural heritage, cultural property, and cultural patrimony. Many of the issues of policy and law that have dominated that debate were resolved by the passage of NAGPRA and, therefore, are no longer central to the resolution of these Native American issues. To explore these issues in greater detail, see Leonard DuBoff, ed., *Art Law: Domestic and International* (South Hackensack, New Jersey: F. B. Rothman, 1975); Paul Bator, *The International Trade in Art* (Chicago: University of Chicago Press, 1983); Bonnie Burnham and the International Council of Museums, *The Protection of Cultural Property: Handbook of National Legislations* (Paris, France: International Council of Museums; dist. by the Tunisian National committee of ICOM, 1974); Leonard DuBoff, *Art Law in a Nutshell* (St. Paul, Minnesota: West Pub. Co., 1984); Leonard DuBoff, *The Deskbook of Art Law* (Washington, D.C.: Federal

Publications, 1977); John Merryman and Albert Elsen, *Law, Ethics and the Visual Arts: Cases and Materials* (New York: Bender, 1979); Karl Meyer, *The Plundered Past* (New York: Atheneum, 1973); Houdek, *Protection of Cultural Property and Archaeological Resources*; Lyndel V. Prott and Patrick J. O'Keefe, *Law and the Cultural Heritage* (Abingdon, Oxfordshire: Professional Books, Ltd., 1984); Sharon A. Williams, *The International and National Protection of Movable Cultural Property: A Comparative Study* (Dobbs Ferry, New York: Oceana Publications, 1978); Gael Graham, "Protection and Reversion of Cultural Property: Issues of Definition and Justification," *International Law* 21 (1987), 755–93; John H. Merryman, "The Retention of Cultural Property," *University of California, Davis Law Review* 21 (1988), 477–93; James A. R. Nafziger, "Protection of Cultural Property," *California Western International Law Journal* 17 (1987), 283; James A. R. Nafziger, "Repose Legislation: A Threat to the Protection of the World's Cultural Heritage," *California Western International Law Journal* 17 (1987), 250; John Petrovich, "The Recovery of Stolen Art: Of Paintings, Statues and Statutes of Limitations," *University of California at Los Angeles Law Review* 27 (1980), 1122; Linda Pinkerton, "Due Diligence in Fine Art Transactions," *Case Western Reserve Journal of International Law* 22 (1990), 1; Deborah Hoover, "Title Disparities in the Art Market: An Emergency Duty of Care for Art Merchants," *George Washington Law Review* 51 (1983) 443n.

34. MacEwan, *Tatanga Mani*, 181.

35. 136 Cong. Rec. H10991 (daily ed. Oct. 22, 1990) (statement of Rep. Mink).

CHAPTER 7 AS YOU WILL: THROUGH THE LOOKING GLASS OF INDIAN LAW AND POLICY, OR, THE CHALLENGE OF PAINTING ON AN UNFINISHED CANVAS

1. See, generally, Rennard Strickland, "Friends and Enemies of the American Indian: An Essay Review on Native American Law and Public Policy," *American Indian Law Review* 3 (1975), 313–31 and sources cited therein.

2. An illustration of the Osage protest document is found in Rennard Strickland, *The Indians in Oklahoma* (Norman: University of Oklahoma Press, 1980), 29.

3. See, generally, *Lyng v. Northwest Indian Cemetery Protective Ass'n*, 485 U.S. 439 (1988); *Brendale v. Confederated Tribes and Bands of the Yakima Indian Nation*, 492 U.S. 408 (1989); *Employment Div. v. Smith*, 494 U.S. 872 (1990); *Duro v. Reina*, 495 U.S. 696 (1990).

4. *Worcester v. Georgia*, 31 U.S. (6Pet.) 515 (1832).

5. *Cherokee Nation v. Oklahoma*, 397 U.S. 620 (1970).

6. Such statements were most often "ceremonial address" and did not, in fact, reflect an inability to understand or a willingness to be directed by the president. The Cherokee removal struggle is a classic example of conflict, and presidential forces.

7. Thomas Fall, *The Ordeal of Running Standing* (New York: Bantam Books, 1971), 193–97. The book has been reissued in a special paperback edition by the University of Oklahoma Press.

8. For example, the American Society of International Law and the United States In-

stitute of Human Rights has sponsored a panel on "The Rights of Indigenous People: A Comparative Analysis," with speakers from Canada, Mexico, and the United States. Several native groups have also recently petitioned the United Nations. See S. James Anoya, *Indigenous People in International Law* (New York: Oxford University Press, 1996).

9. See Angie Debo, *And Still the Waters Run: The Betrayal of the Five Civilized Tribes* (Princeton: Princeton University Press, 1940).

10. Gerald A. Reed, "Financial Controversy in the Cherokee Nation, 1839–1846," *Chronicles of Oklahoma* 52:1 (1974), 82–98.

11. Jack Gregory and Rennard Strickland, *Adventures of an Indian Boy* (Muskogee: Indian Heritage Association, 1971).

12. John Stands In Timber and Margot Liberty, *Cheyenne Memories* (New Haven: Yale University Press, 1967), 272–74.

13. See, generally, Felix Cohen, *Federal Indian Law* (Albuquerque: University of New Mexico Press, 1971), with special reference to the Foreword by Robert L. Bennett and Frederick M. Hart.

14. See Rennard Strickland, "Redeeming Centuries of Dishonor: Legal Education and the American Indian," *Toledo Law Review* (1970), 847; and Rennard Strickland, "Educating Indian Lawyers Is Not Enough," *Student Lawyer* 17 (1972), 4–9.

15. An especially fine biography exploring the problems faced by an Indian lawyer more than a century ago is W. David Baird, *Peter Pitchlynn: Chief of the Choctaws* (Norman: University of Oklahoma Press, 1972). See also Chapter One, here, on John Rollin Ridge, the first Native admitted to the practice of law in California.

16. Rennard Strickland, unpublished Osage field notes, in the author's personal possession.

AFTERWORD   STRANGERS   IN   A   STRANGE   LAND:
PERSONAL   AND   HISTORICAL   REFLECTIONS

1. David Farmer and Rennard Strickland (comps.), *A Trumpet of Our Own: Yellow Bird's Essays on the North American Indian* (San Francisco: Book Club of California, 1981), 22, 31.

2. 15 Stat. 581 (1868).

3. General Allotment (Dawes) Act, ch. 119, 24 Stat. 388 (1887) (codified as amended in scattered sections of 25 U.S.C.).

4. Althea Bass and Carl Sweezy, *The Arapaho Way: A Memoir of an Indian Boy* (New York: C. N. Potter, 1966), 50.

5. Will and Ariel Durant, *The Lessons of History* (New York: Simon and Schuster, 1968), 37–42.

6. See, generally, Rennard Strickland, "The Lawyer as Modern Medicine Man," *Southern Illinois University Law Journal* 11 (1986), 302.

7. Alexis de Tocqueville, *Democracy in America*, trans. Francis Bowen (1862), ed. Phillips Bradley (New York: Alfred A. Knopf, 1945), 1:277.

8. Christopher Columbus Langdell, the dean of Harvard Law School in the late nineteenth century, proclaimed in 1871 that the study of law was a science and that the library

was a laboratory in which we dissect cases like biology experiments. For a discussion of Langdell's view of law as science, see Robert Stevens, *Law School: Legal Education in America from the 1850s to the 1980s* (Chapel Hill: University of North Carolina Press, 1983), 52–53.

9. See, generally, Robert A. Williams, Jr., *The American Indian in Western Legal Thought: The Discourses of Conquest* (New York: Oxford University Press, 1990).

10. Hugh Honour, *The New Golden Land: European Images of America from the Discoveries to the Present Time* (New York: Pantheon Books, 1975), 12.

11. Ibid., 8.

12. Ibid., 12.

13. Ibid., 10.

14. The Chatty Kathy doll was a popular children's toy that recited a pre-recorded message when her string was pulled. For a more detailed development of these ideas, see Rennard Strickland, "Inventing the Indian Doll: Observations of an Indian Lawyer about Law and Native Americans," *Virginia Law School Report* 5 (1981), 6.

15. Barbara W. Tuchman, *Practicing History: Selected Essays* (New York: Knopf, 1981), 289.

16. For revised estimates of losses, see Russell Thornton, "The Demography of the Trail of Tears: A New Estimate of Cherokee Population Losses," in William L. Anderson (ed.), *Cherokee Removal: Before and After* (Athens: University of Georgia Press, 1991), 75, 75–76.

17. See Rennard Strickland, "Genocide-At-Law: An Historic and Contemporary View of the Native American Experience," *Kansas Law Review* 34 (1986), 713. The argument of the essay is that the law was used as a tool of extermination, as illustrated by a Georgia law that placed Indians beyond the protection of the law, or as a tool of culturecide or geographical relocation which produced death. Ibid., 720–21. Note the use of the Courts of Indian Offense and the outlawing of the Sun Dance and the lottery as devices to redistribute lands. Ibid., 728.

18. Tocqueville, *Democracy in America*, 1:354–55.

19. Angie Debo, *And Still the Waters Run: The Betrayal of the Five Civilized Tribes* (Princeton: Princeton University Press, 1940), ix–x.

20. Felix Cohen, "The Erosion of Indian Rights, 1950–53: A Case Study in Bureaucracy," *Yale Law Journal* 62 (1953) 349, 390.

21. *Oliphant v. The Suquamish Indian Tribe*, 435 U.S. 191, 206 (1978).

22. Hagan based this conclusion not only upon his extensive scholarly research in libraries, but upon his years of working with Native peoples in upstate New York and later in Oklahoma. It is not just the numbers that speak of survival, it is the lifeway as well!

23. For elaboration of this statistical data and citations thereto, see, generally, Rennard Strickland, "Indian Law and the Miner's Canary: The Signs of Poison Gas," *Cleveland State Law Review* 39 (1991).

24. James Welch, *The Indian Lawyer* (New York: W. W. Norton and Co., 1990), 51.

25. Ibid., 53–54.

26. See, generally, Rennard Strickland and Margaret Archeleta, et. al., *Shared Visions: Native American Painters and Sculptors in the Twentieth Century* (Phoenix, Arizona: Heard Museum, 1991).

27. See Rennard Strickland, "To Do the Right Things: Cherokee Traditions of Justice

under Law," *American Indian Law Review* 17 (1992), 337, 339–340; see also Alexander Solzhenitsyn, *Warning to the Western World* (London: Bodley Head: British Broadcasting Corporation, 1976), 45, where Solzhenitsyn declares that "at the present time it is widely accepted among lawyers that law is higher than morality."

28. Patty Harjo, "Who Am I?", in Jeannette Henry, ed., *The American Indian Reader* (San Francisco: Indian Historian Press, 1973), 113.

29. Rennard Strickland, *The Indians in Oklahoma* (Norman: University of Oklahoma Press, 1980), 115.

30. Ibid., 116.

31. Ibid., 117.

32. R. J. Forbes, *The Conquest of Nature* (New York: Praeger, 1968), 92.

33. See Loren Eiseley, "The Hidden Teacher," in *The Unexpected Universe* (New York: Harcourt, Brace & World, 1969), 48.

34. Ibid., 51.

35. Ibid., 56. Eiseley also noted that "nature is full of traps for the beast that cannot learn." Ibid., 55.

36. Ibid., 64.

37. For the quotation from Ortega y Gasset's *Modern Theme*, see Strickland, *Indians in Oklahoma*, 118.

38. D. H. Lawrence, "Fenimore Cooper's Leatherstocking Novels," in his *Studies in Classic American Literature* (1923; Garden City, N. Y.: Doubleday and Co. 1953), 55, 60. For more of Lawrence's writing on the American Indian, see Edward D. MacDonald (ed.), *Phoenix: The Posthumous Papers of D. H. Lawrence* (New York: Viking Press, 1964).

39. Harjo, "Who Am I?," 113.

INDEX

Aaron, Paul, 43
Activism, legal, 57–58
Actors, Native American, 36–37. *See also* Film
Adair, John, 36
Age of Discovery, 123
Alaskan Natives, 52; land issues, 59; NAGPRA, 87; reburial and repatriation, 58, 87
American Indian Heritage Association, 31
American Indian Registry of the Performing Arts, 31
Ameringer, Oscar, 13
Anglo-American law, 89
Apache Indians: media images, 19; population, 19
Apted, Michael, 42
Arizona Native American Tourism Center, 34
Art, 63–75, 99–100; Longfish, 47, 61; sacred objects, 92–93
Artists Hopid, 72
Artists Space, 34
Assimilation, forced, 110
Austin Walker v. Dept. of Interior, 60

Backlash against Indians, 101–2
Bedord, Irene, 36
BIA. *See* Bureau of Indian Affairs

Big Bow, Woody, 67
Big Tree (Chief), 37
Black Elk, 126
Black Robe (1991), 41
Bliss, William, 83
Blue deer, 72–75
Blue Eagle, Acee, 67, 75
Bosin, Blackbear, 128
Bowman, Arlene, 35
Brandon, William, 84
Brendale v. Confederated Tribes & Bands of the Yakima Nation, 103
Brown v. Board of Education, 3
Buffalo Meat, 63
Bureau of Indian Affairs (BIA): changes, 61; termination policy, 49–50

Cagney, James, 20
California, 5–9
Calvin Horn lectures, xiii–xiv
Cannon, T.C., 48, 63, 68–69
Carewe, Edwin, 33
Carter, Jimmy, 124–25
Ceremonials, 65
Chandler, Jeff, 21
Chaney, Lon, Jr., 21
Chatty Kathy Indian Doll, 101–2
Cherokee Indians: Indian law, 77–84; population, 19, 52; Southern, 8

149